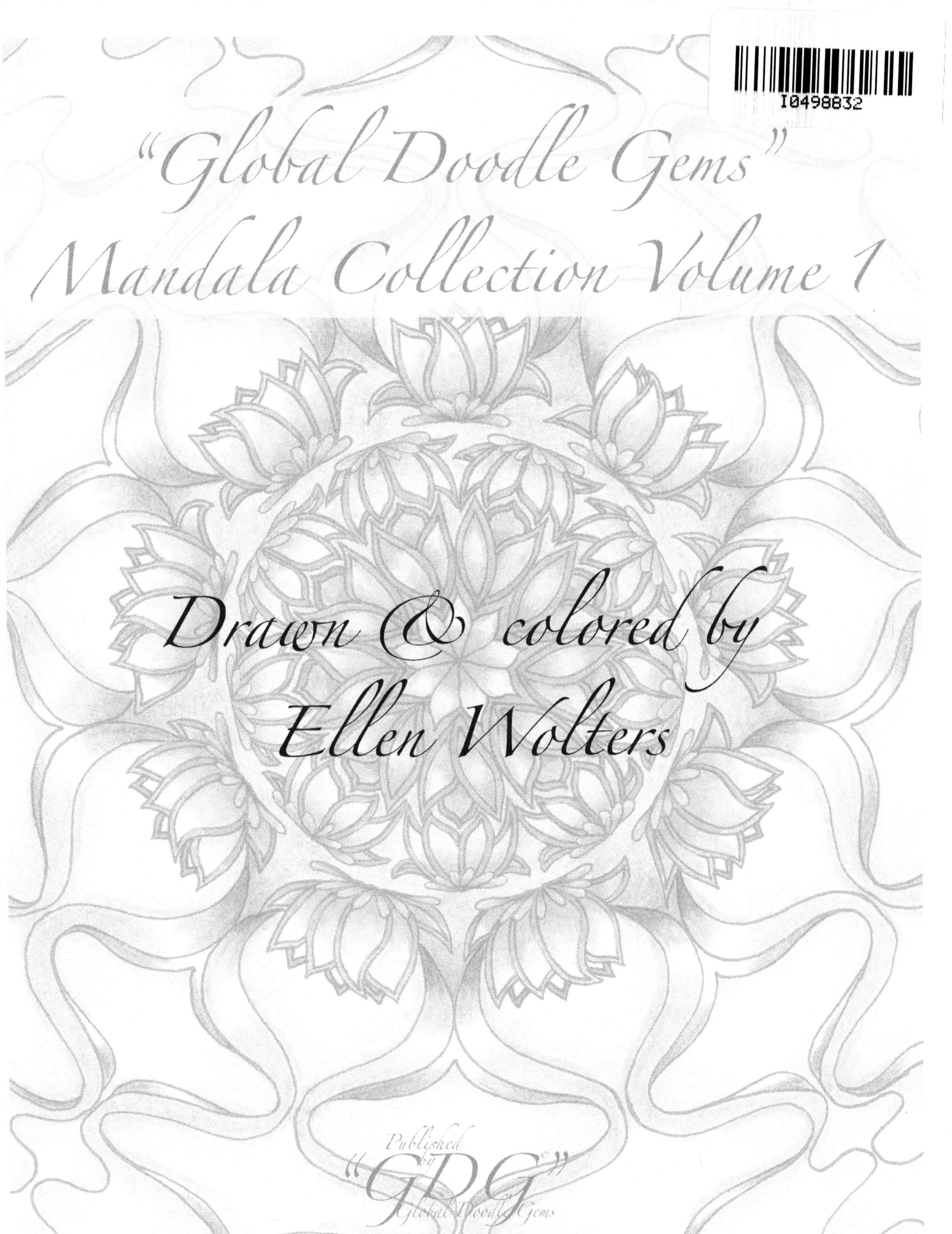

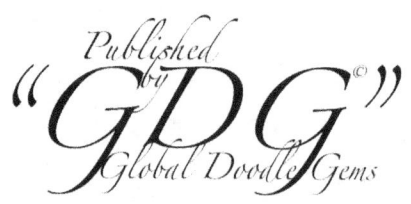

Share your colored versions with us ! We love seeing your results and hearing from you we are social !

The Official FB book page, stay on top of what we have in the works !
www.facebook.com/globaldoodlegems

The Community group, share your colored pages, meet the artists, enjoy exclusive freebies, take part in community Charity books and so much more......
www.facebook.com/groups/globaldoodlegems/

Follow us on Twitter.... @GlobalDoodlegem

We are on Instagram too
@globaldoodlegems for instagram

...and if you are not social like that we have a blog
globaldoodlegems.wordpress.com

Copyright © 2015 Global Doodle Gems

All rights are reserved by Global Doodle Gems.

Duplication of pages for personal use are allowed. You are invited to color the pages then scan/post your coloured versions to social networks, mentioning the book title and author/artist (Global Doodle Gems).

All artwork and images are protected by copyright laws. This book or any portion thereof may not, otherwise, be reproduced and/or distributed or transmitted without the express written permission of the artist/publisher of Global Doodle Gems.

All of us from the Global Doodle Gems wish you a colortastic time and look forward to seeing your wonderful color results online !

Participating Artists

1. Gemeta Ling
2. DomDomx
3. Johanna Ans
4. Lynne McGee
5. TJ
6. Pica Wu
7. Ahmed Fouad
8. Rover
9. Yaya
10. Marieke Raterman-Bos
11. Dawn Miller
12. Audrey Sagh
13. Nicole Whelan
14. Mireille Westerduin, Colour by Mi
15. Ellen Wolters

Contributing Artist
Gemeta Ling
Germany

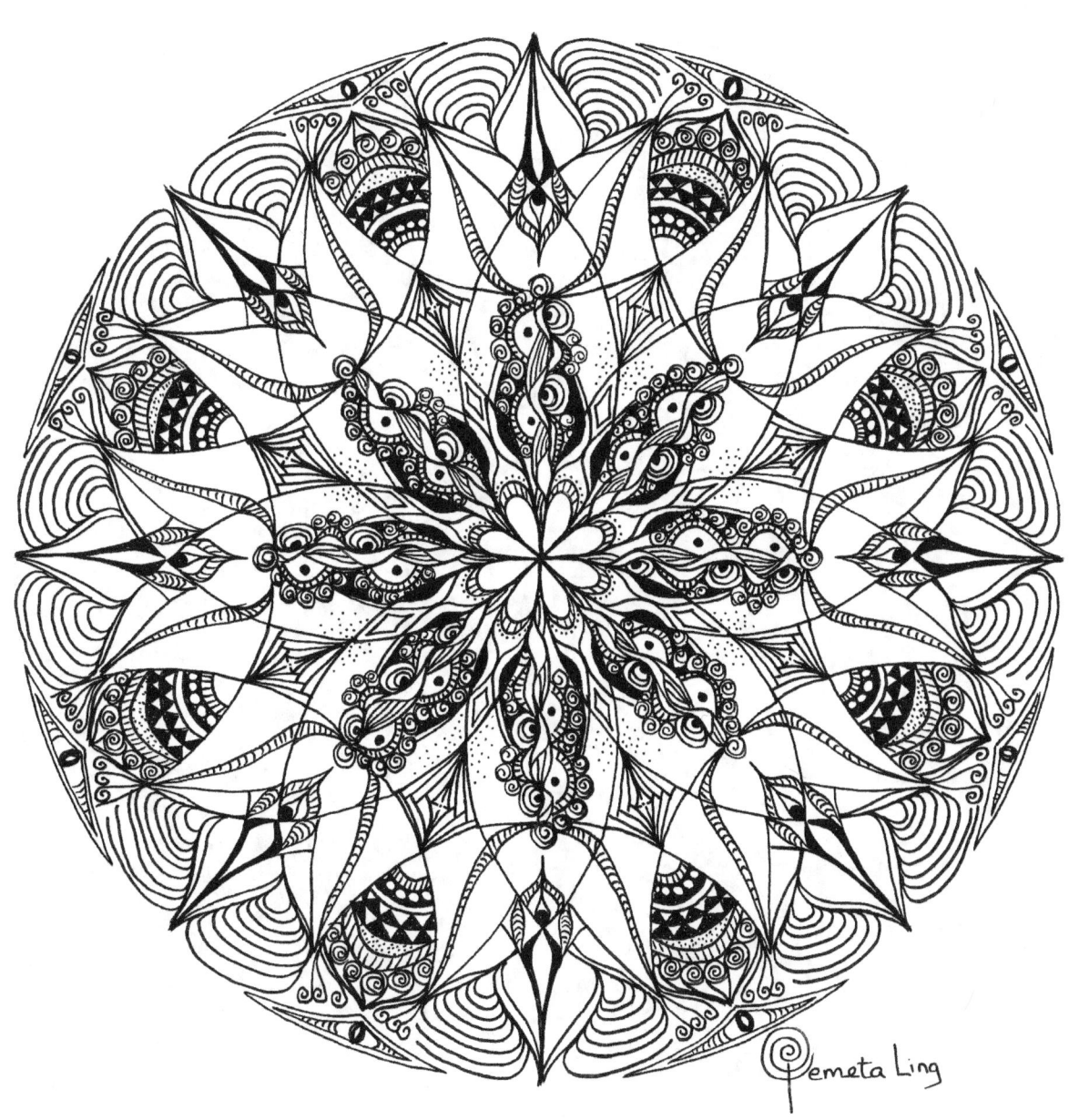

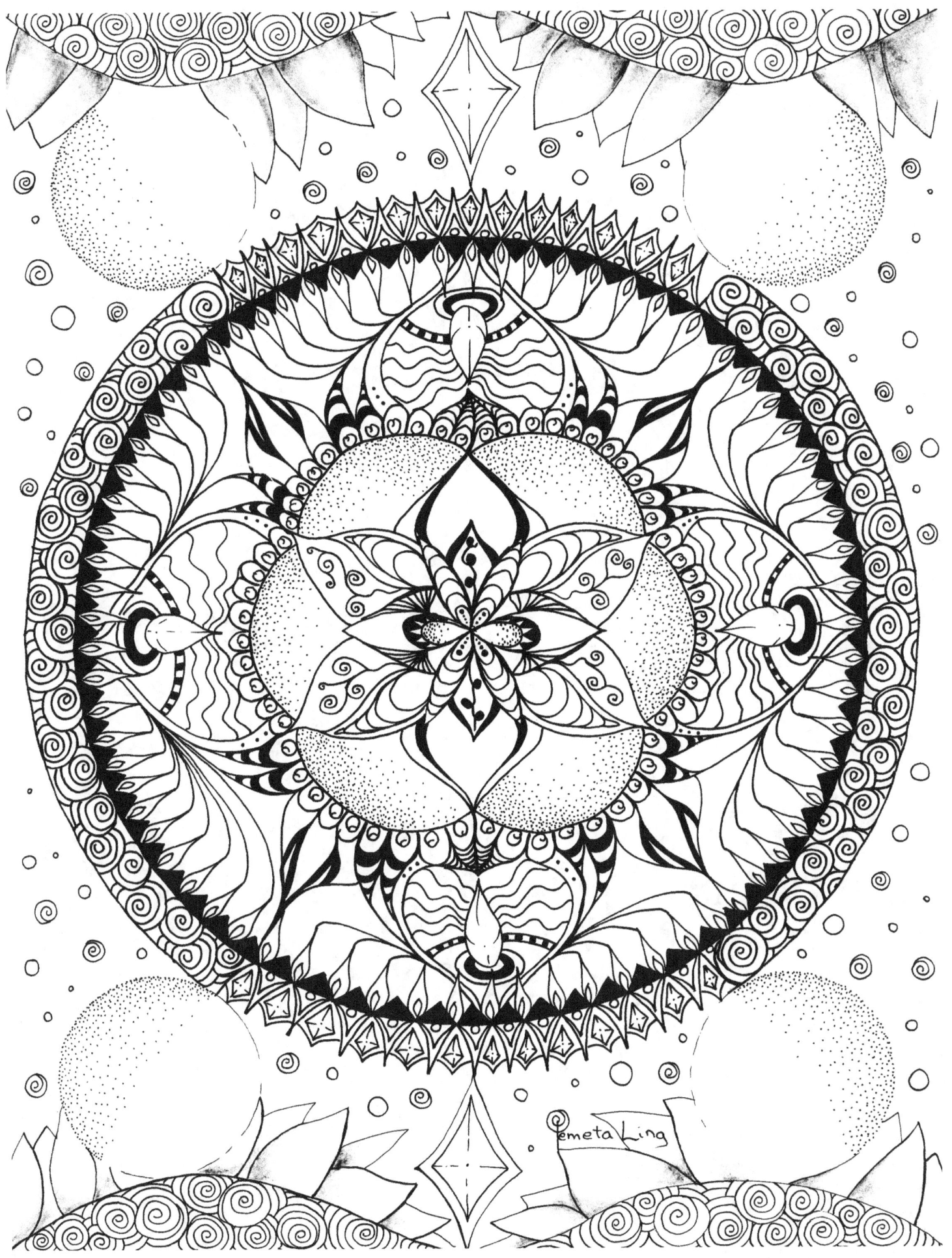

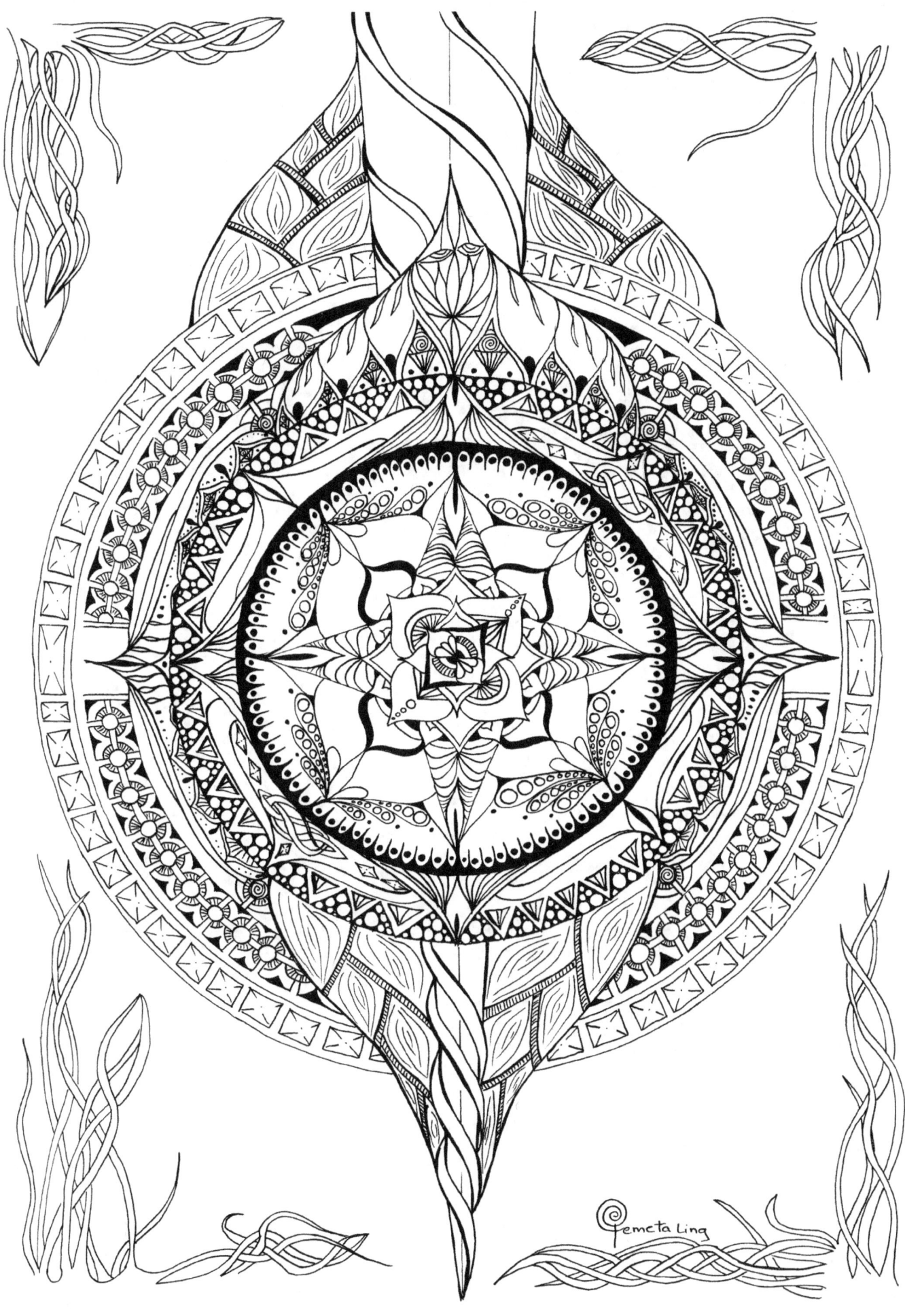

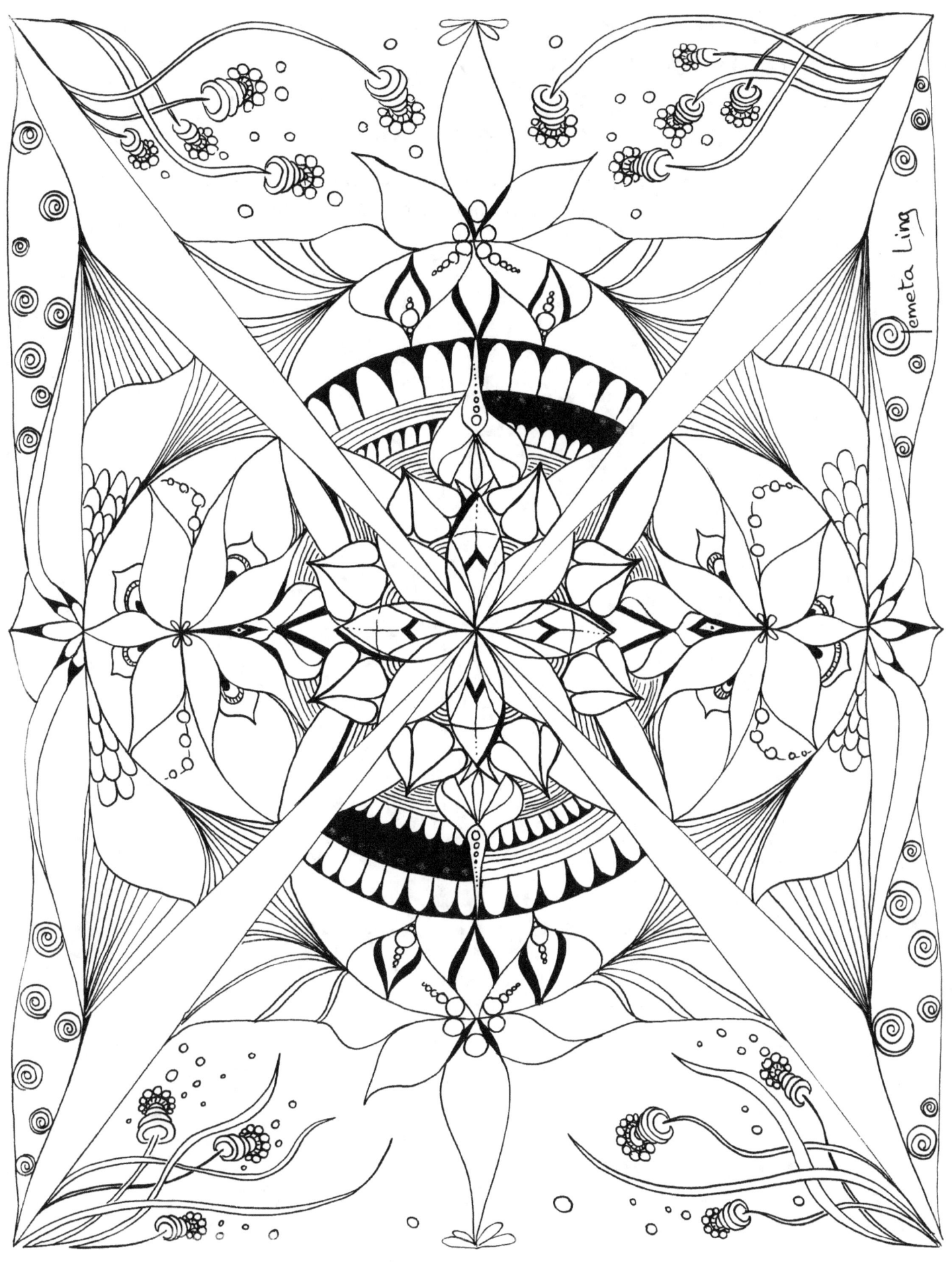

Contributing Artist
DomDomx
France

Facebook : Les-dessins-et-doodles-de-Dom-Domx
Facebook Group : Color.Addict

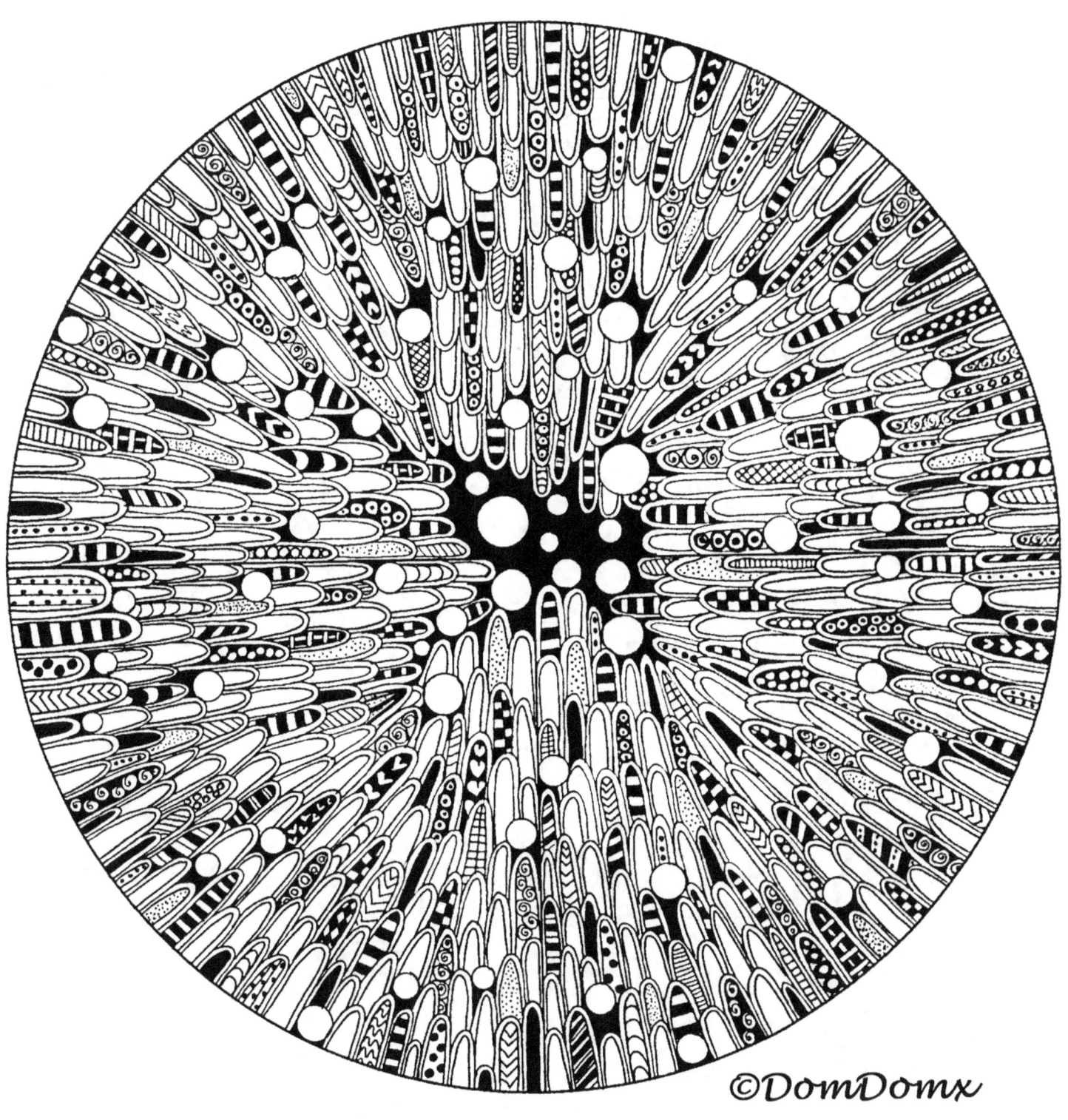

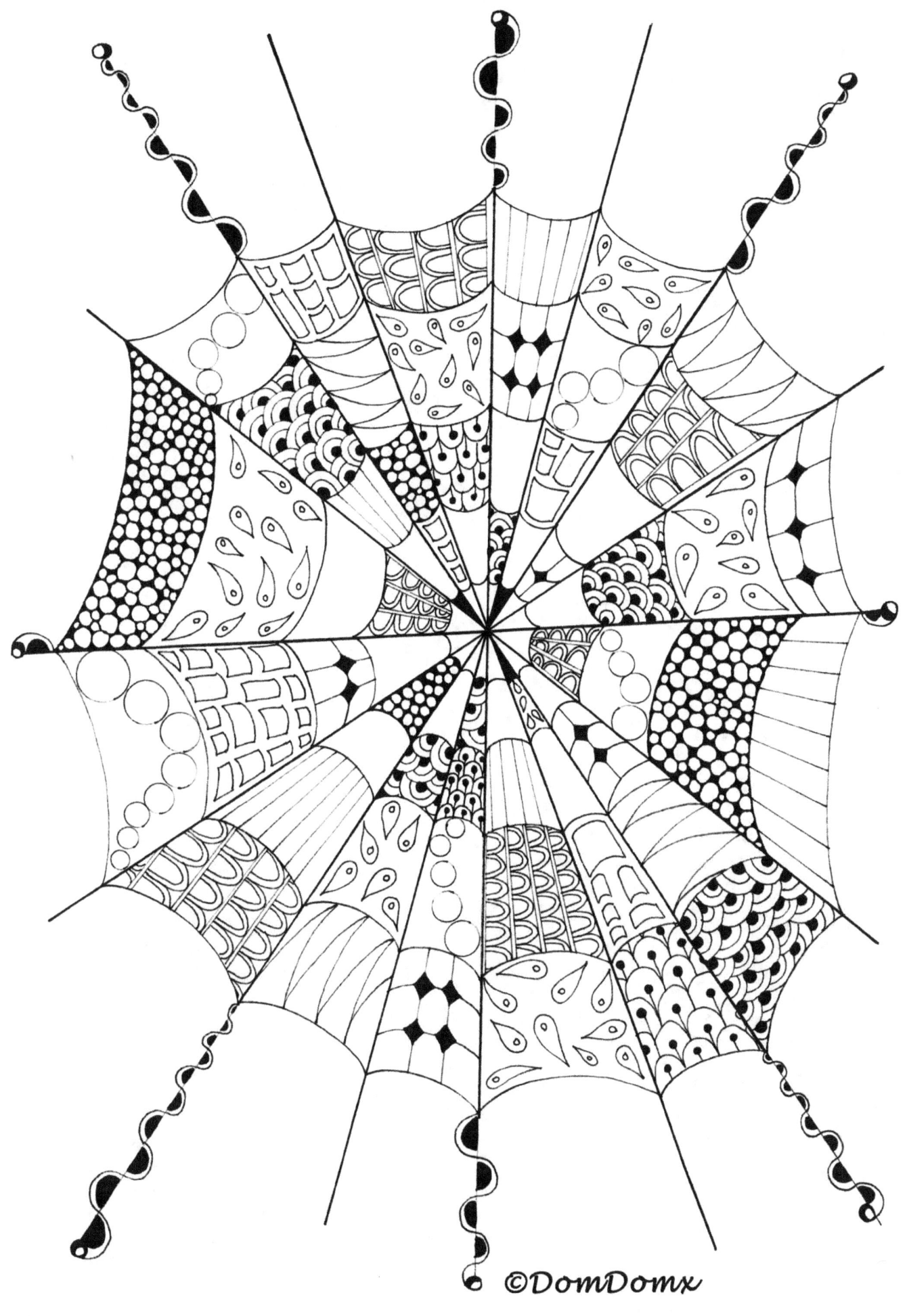

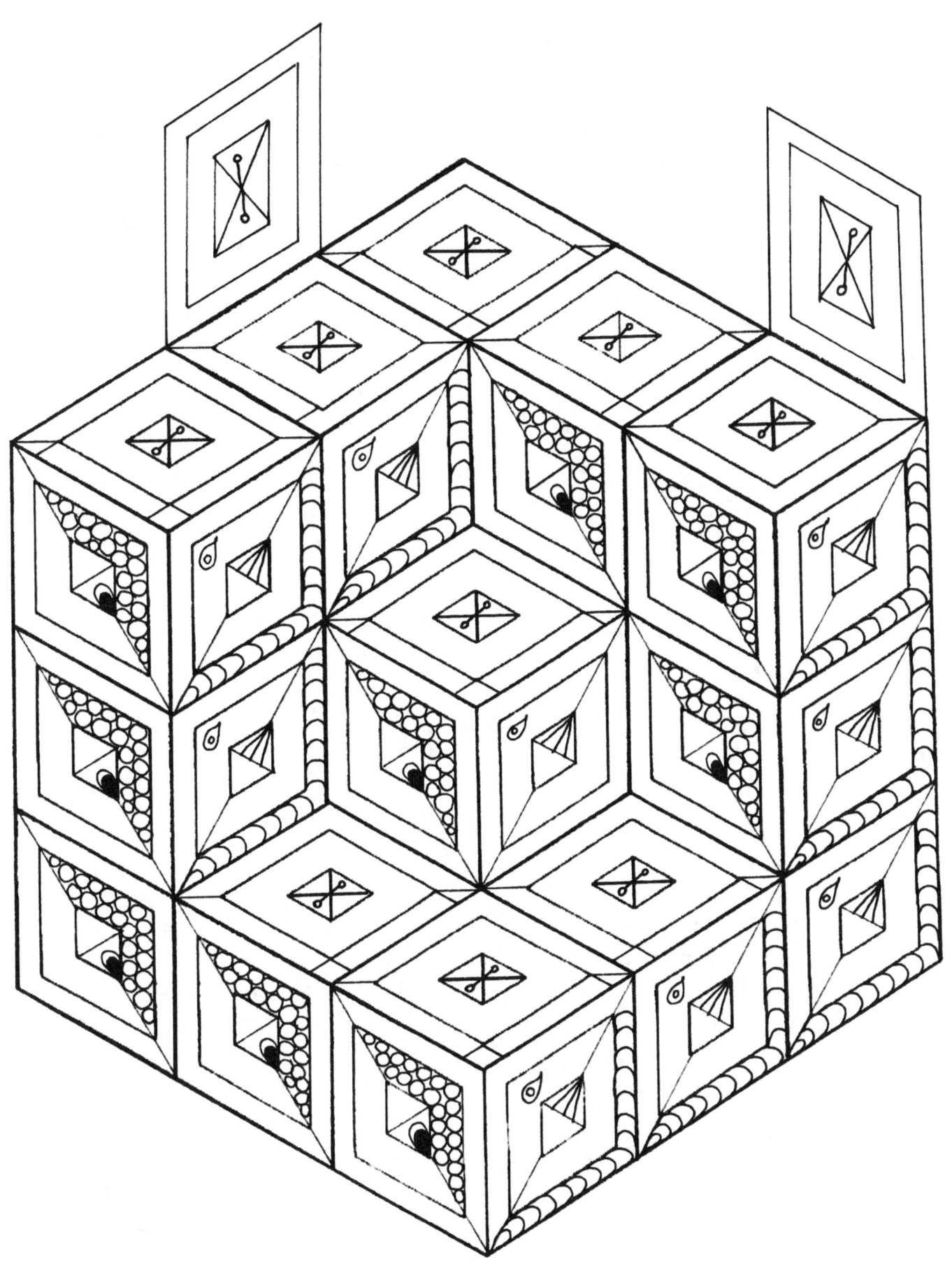

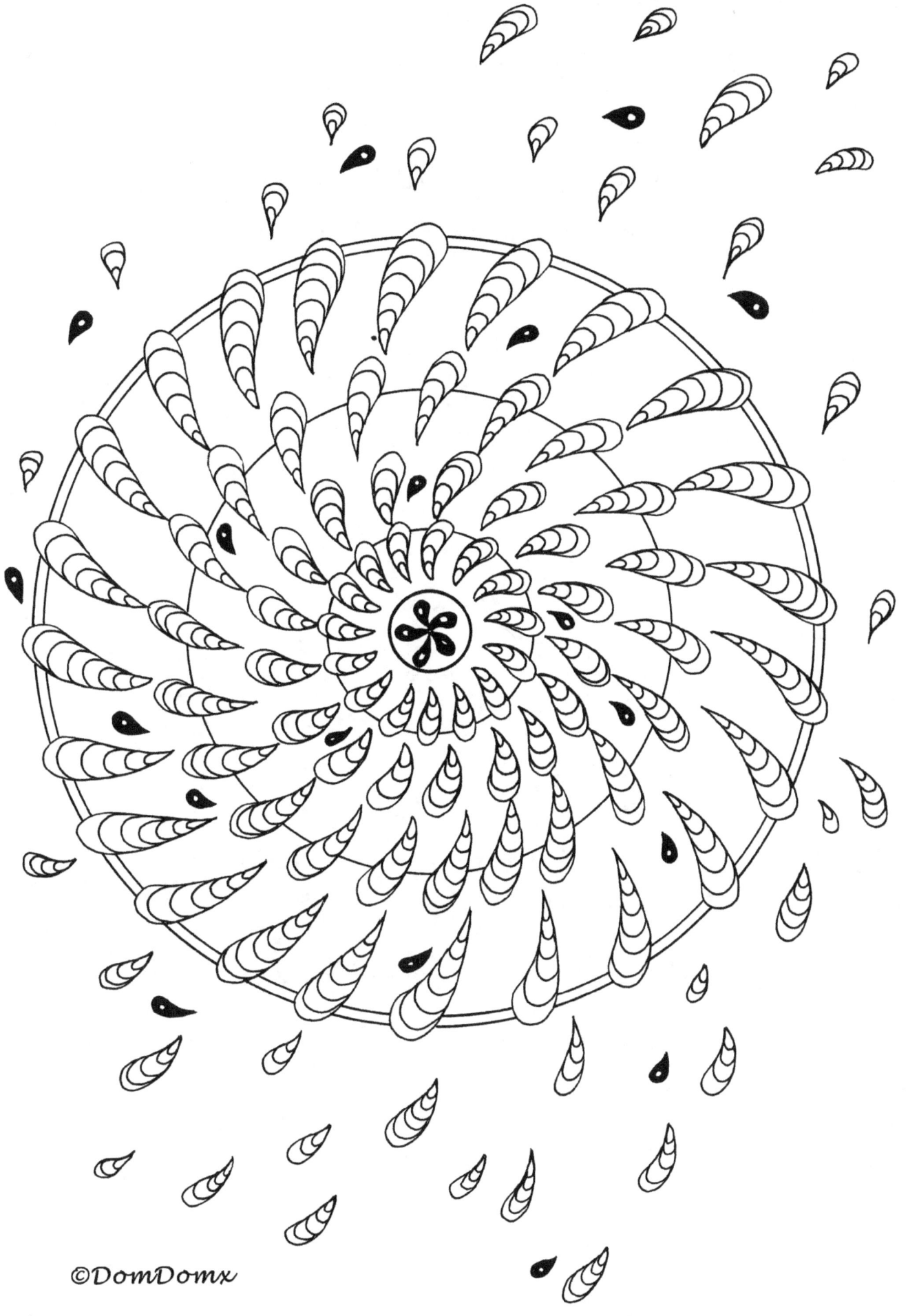

Contributing Artist
MWMS-Johanna Ans
The Netherlands

Blog : mywaymystylejohannaans.wordpress.com

Facebook : Johanna-Ans-My-creative-site

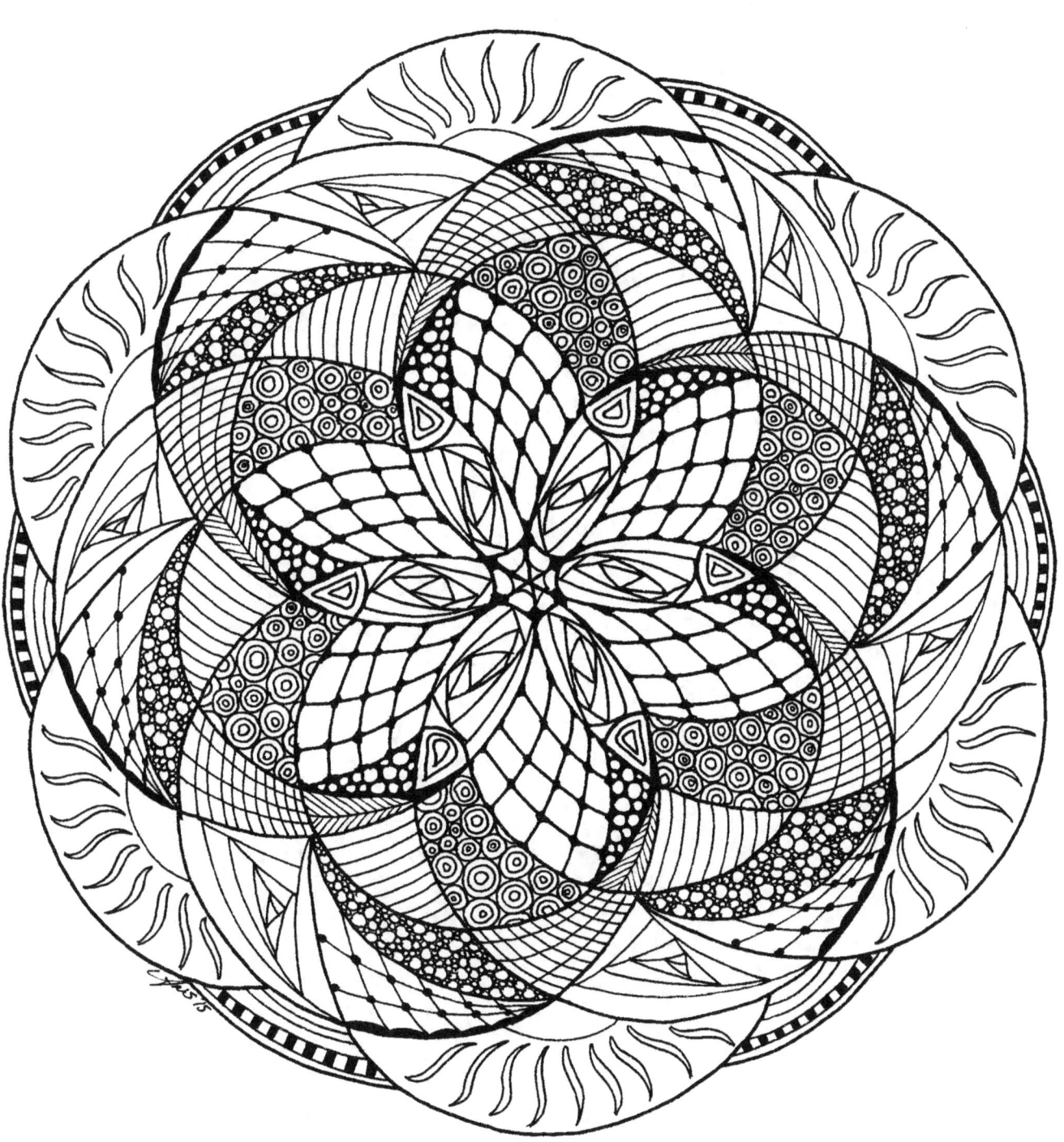

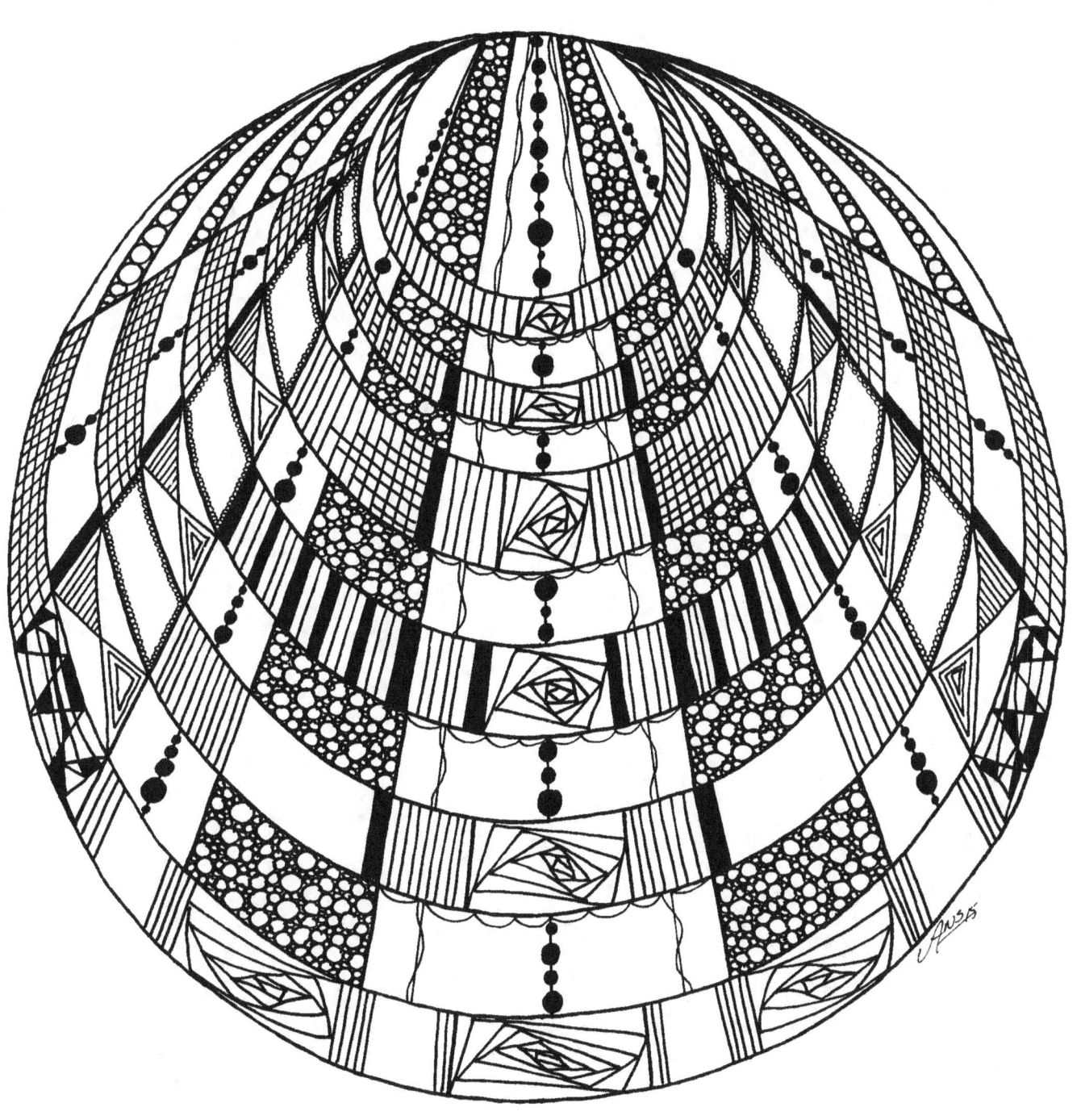

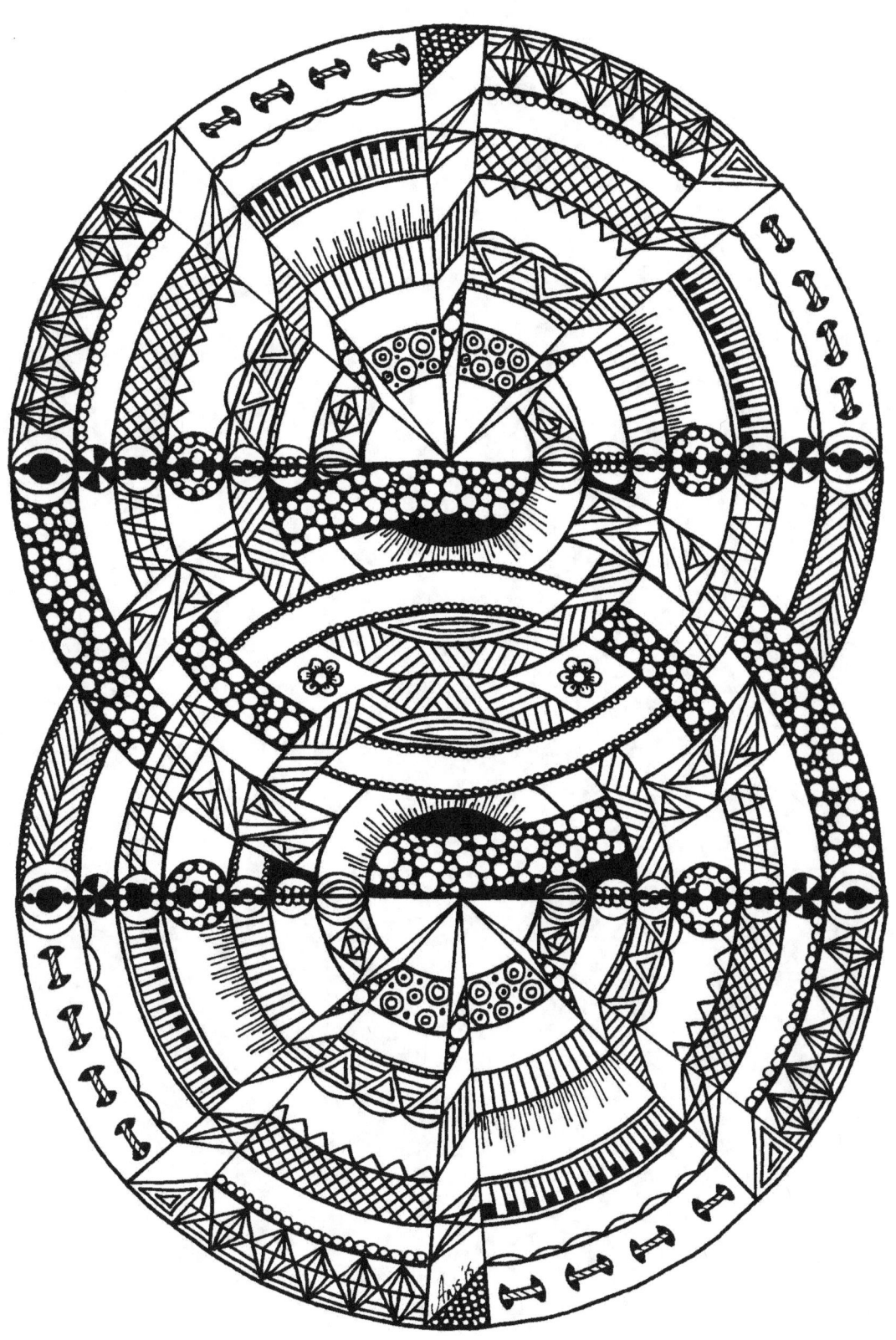

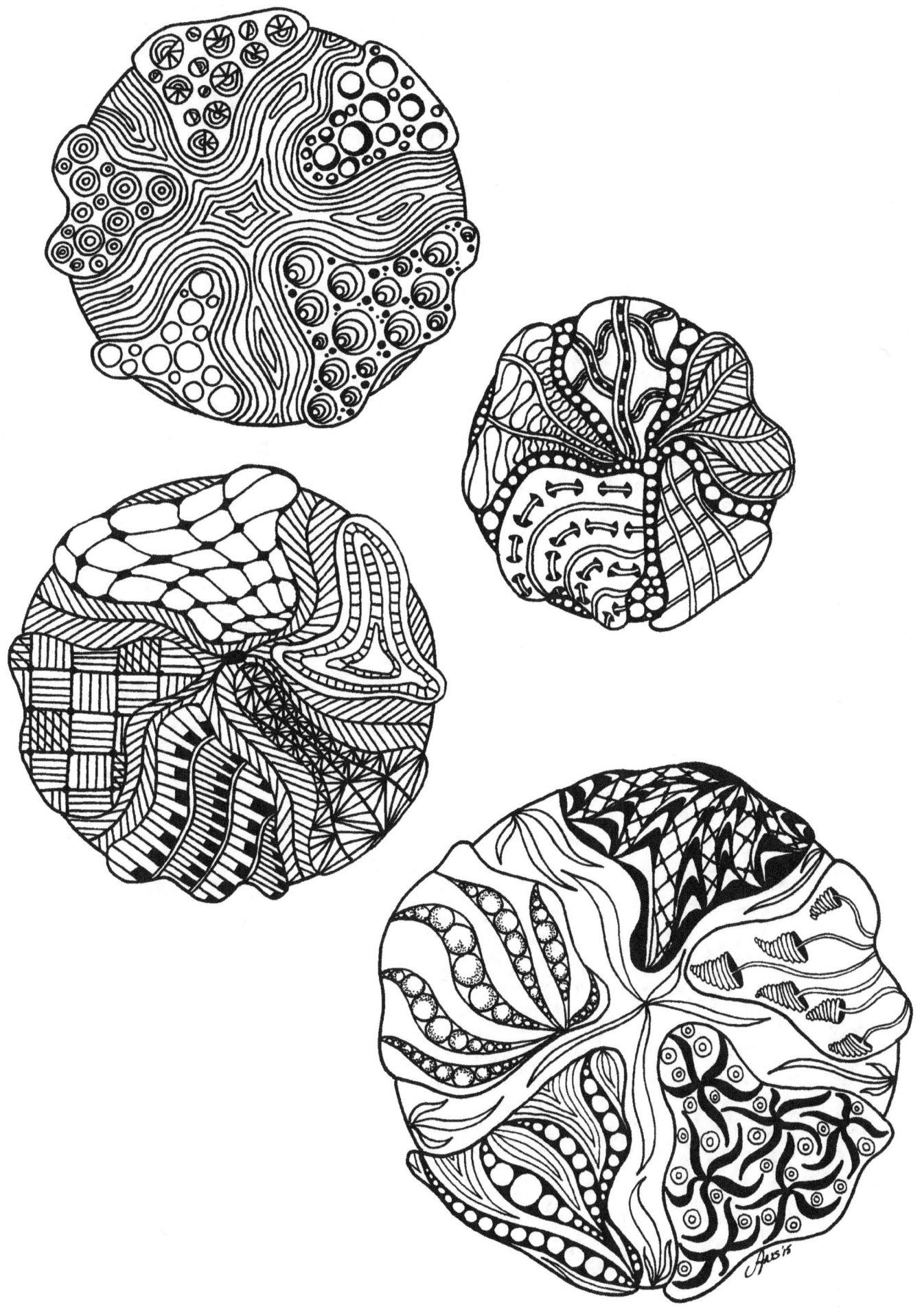

Contributing Artist
Lynne McGee
Brisbane, Australia

Facebook : Colorandtangle

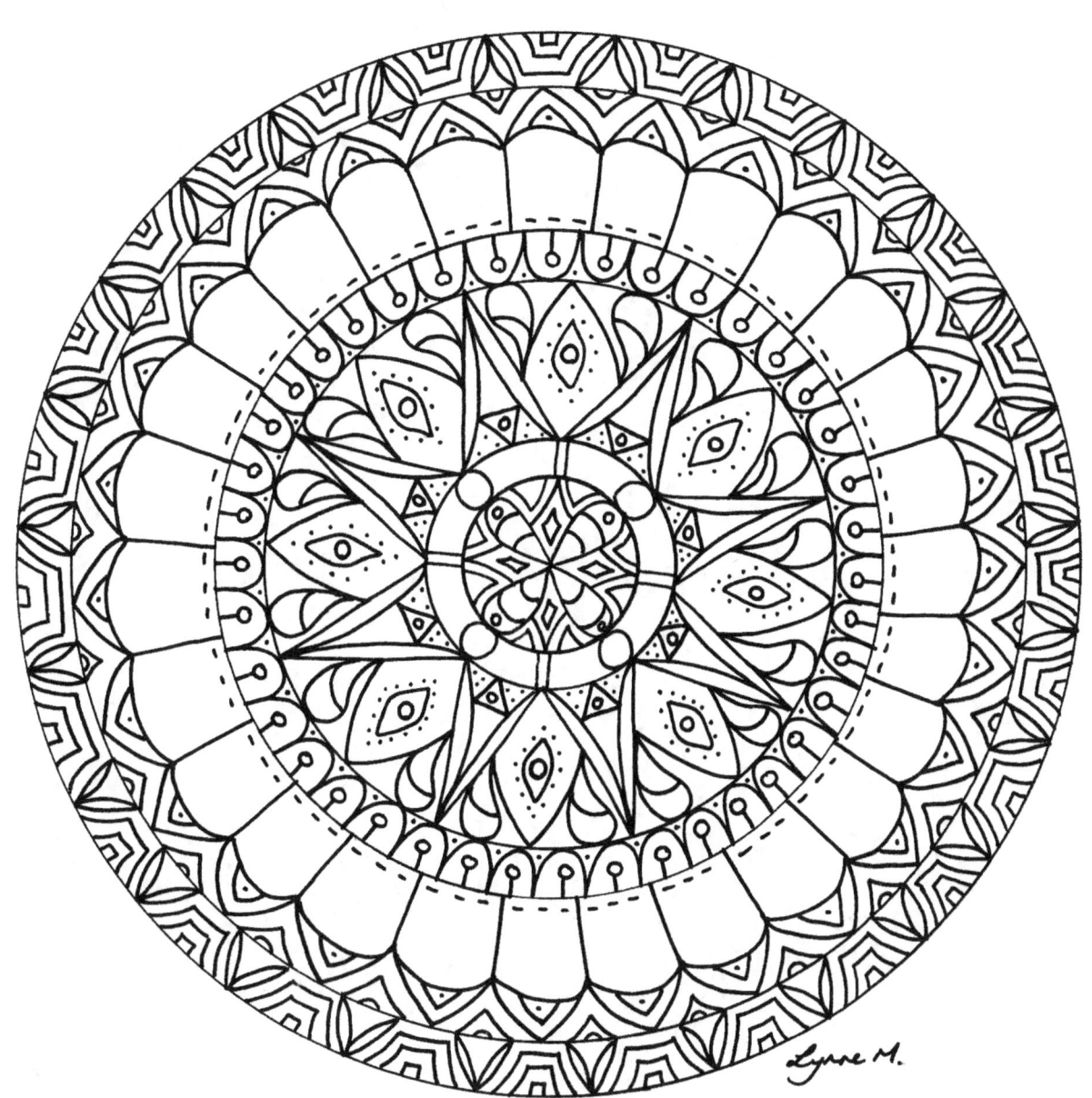

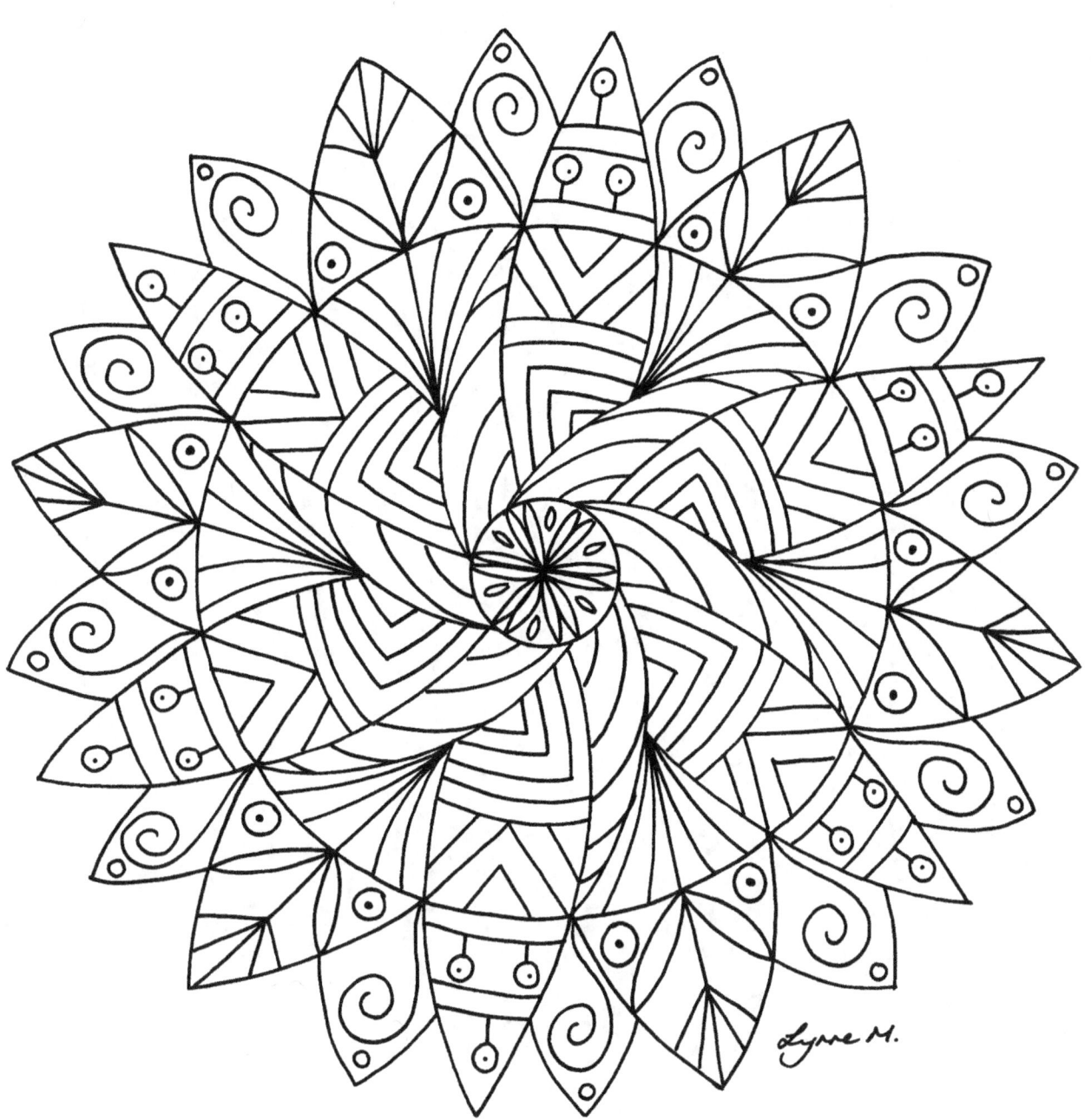

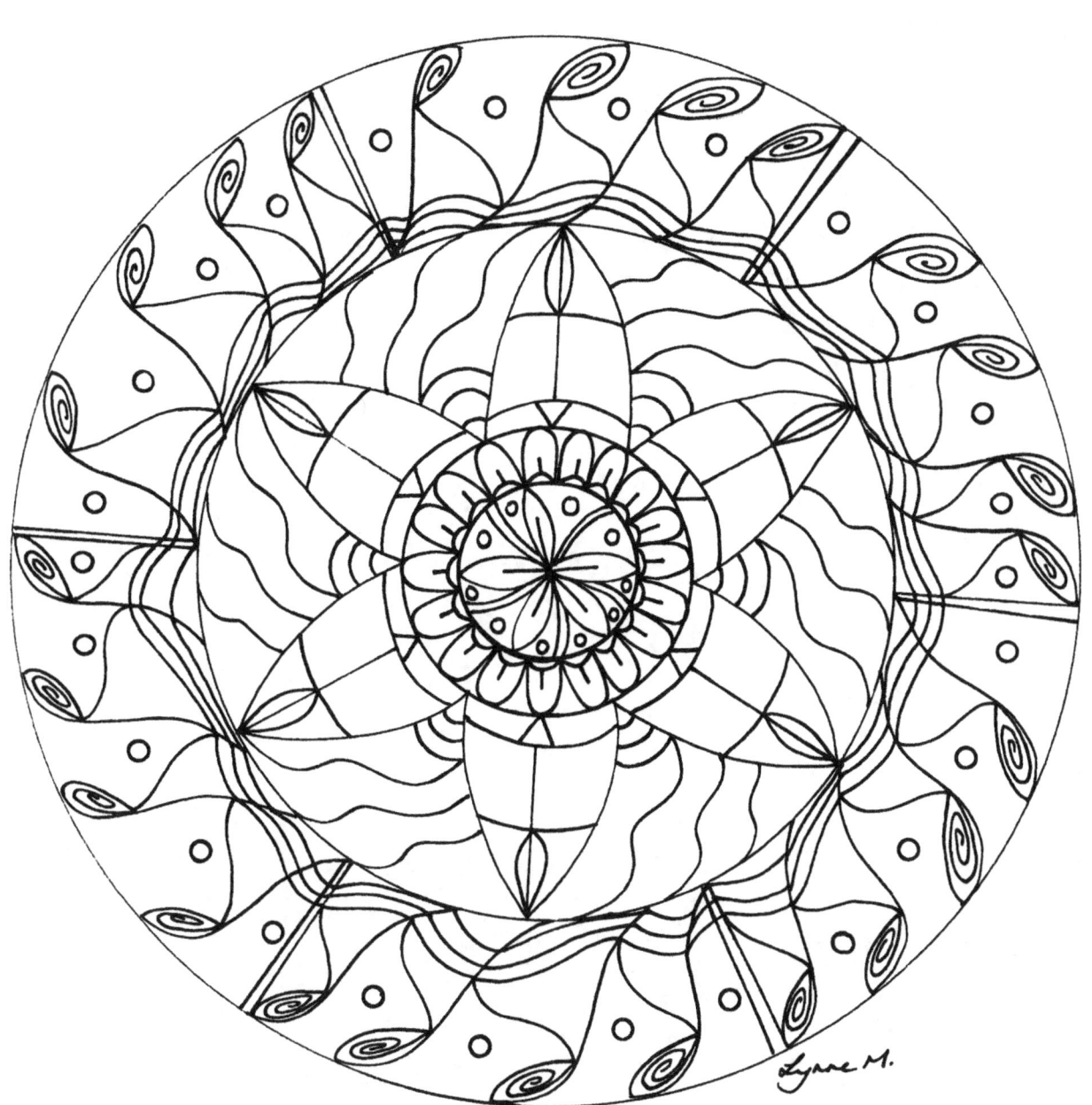

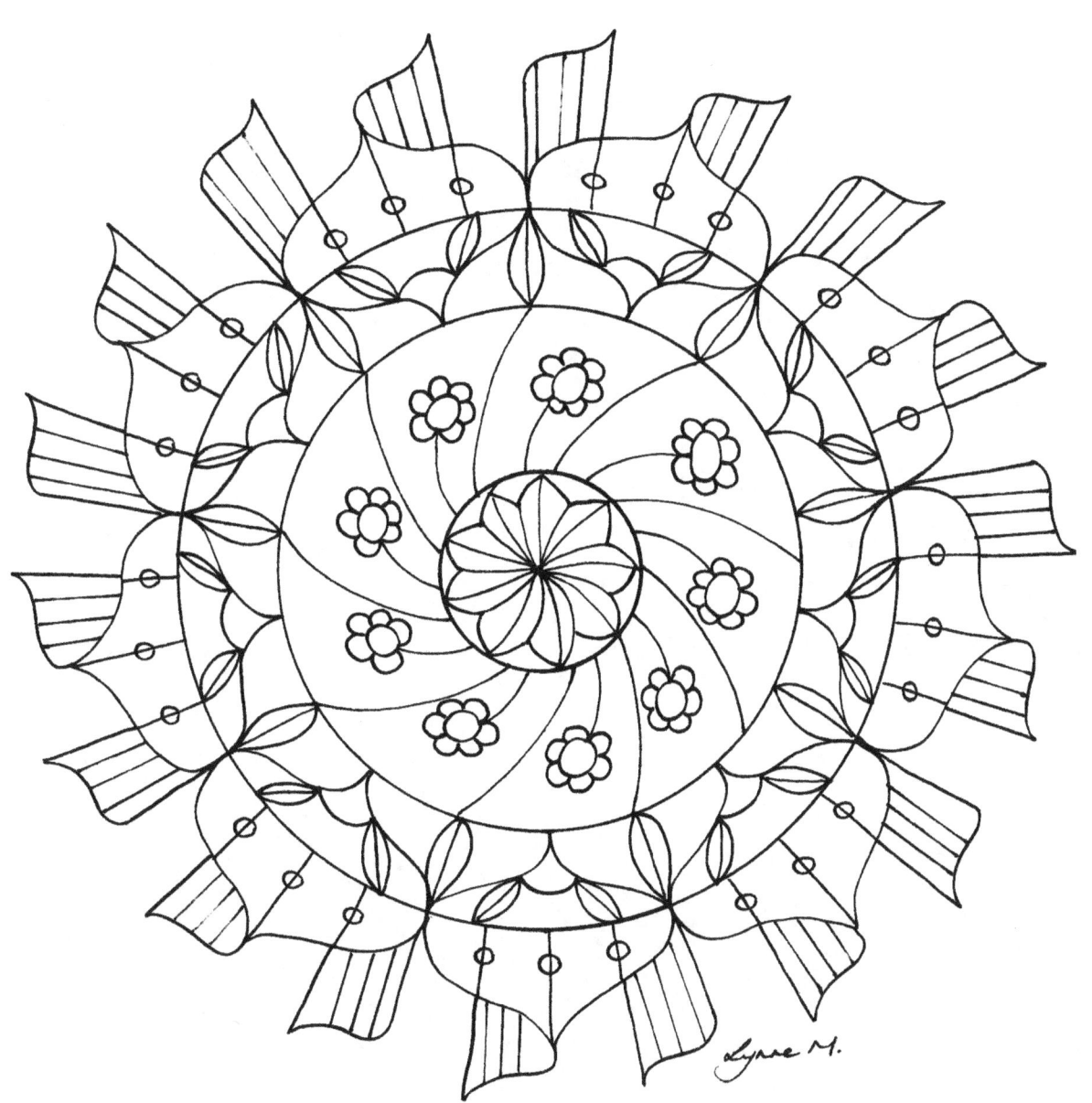

Contributing Artist
T.J.
USA

Facebook : TJsArtCorner

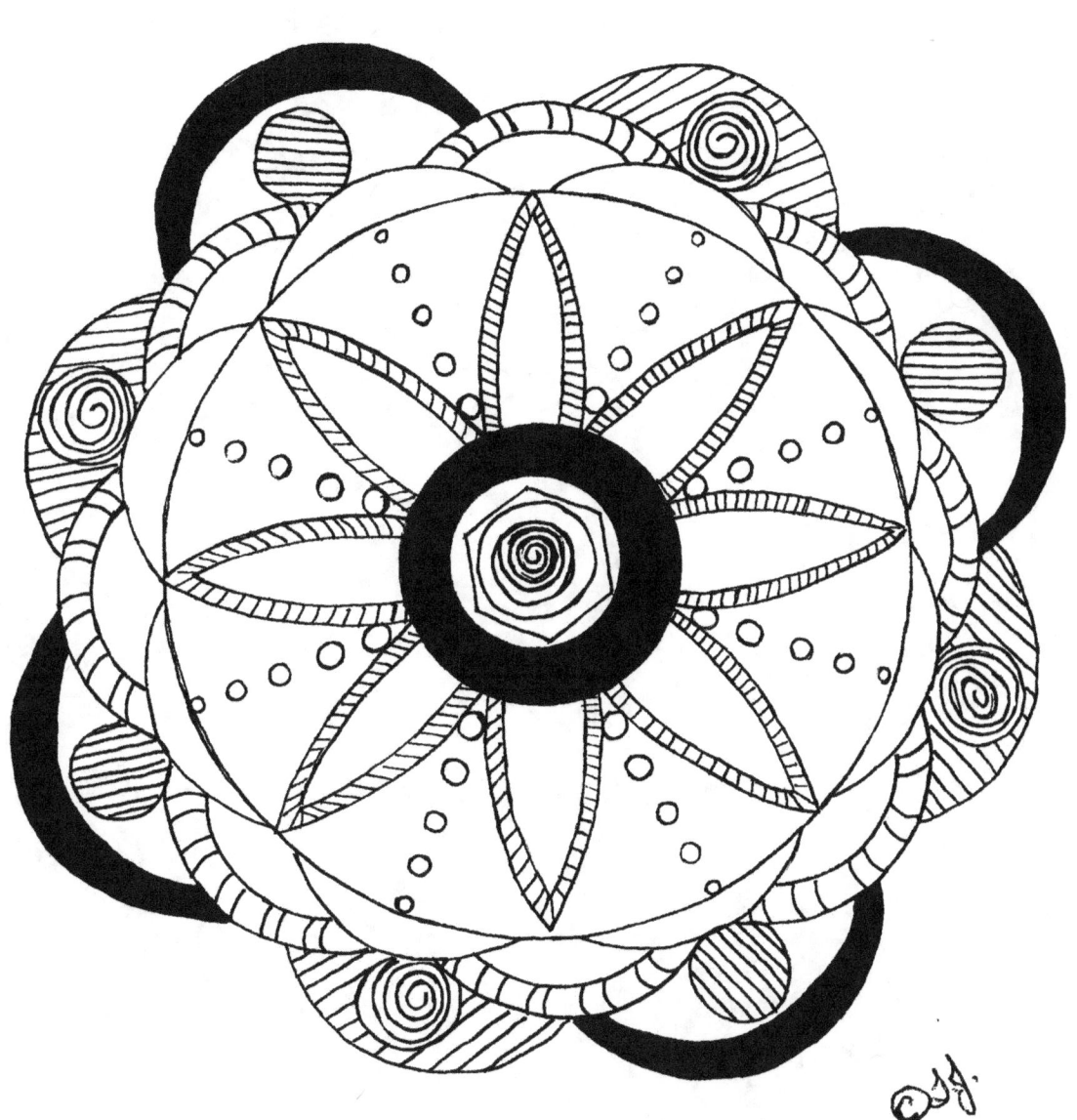

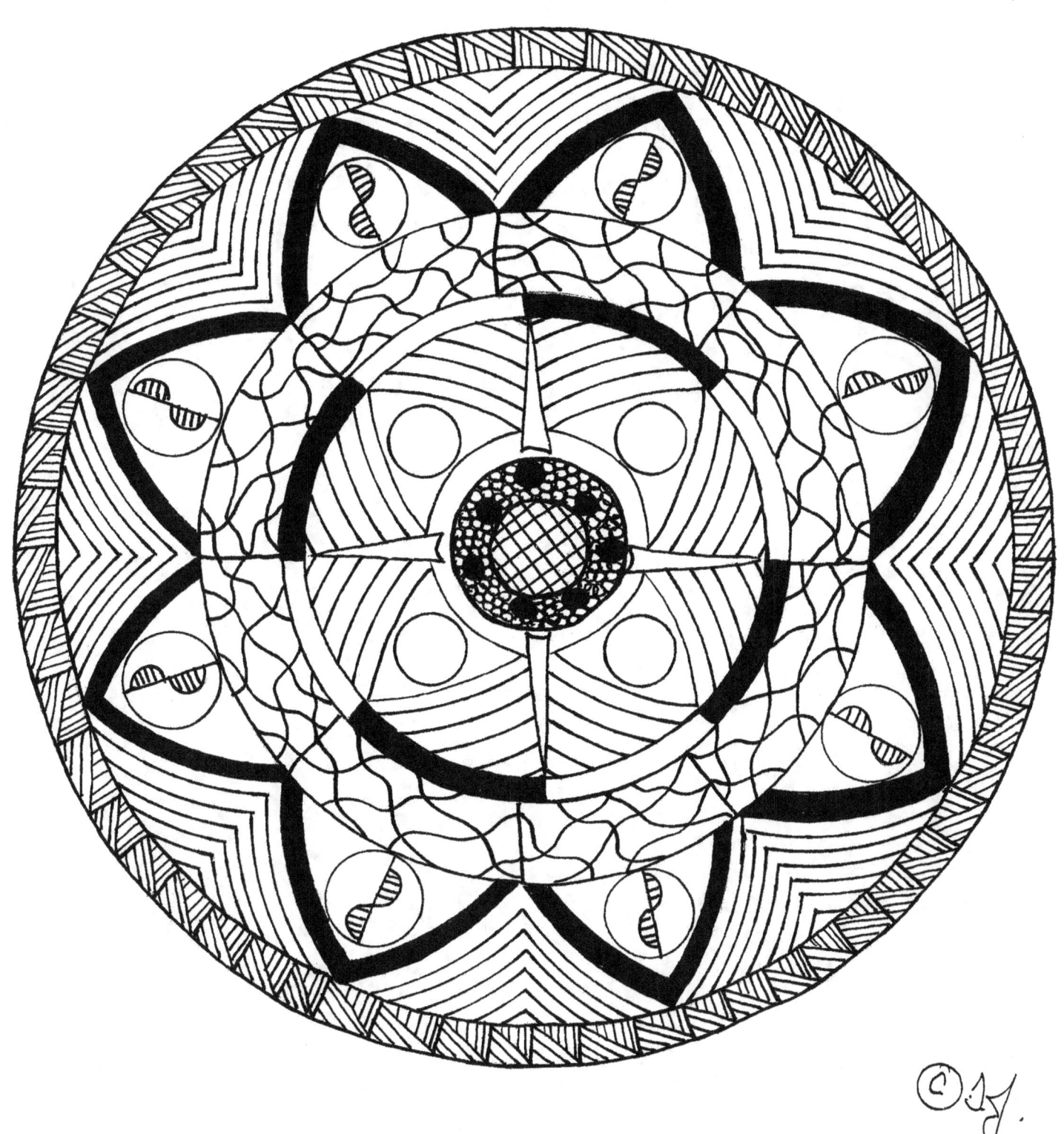

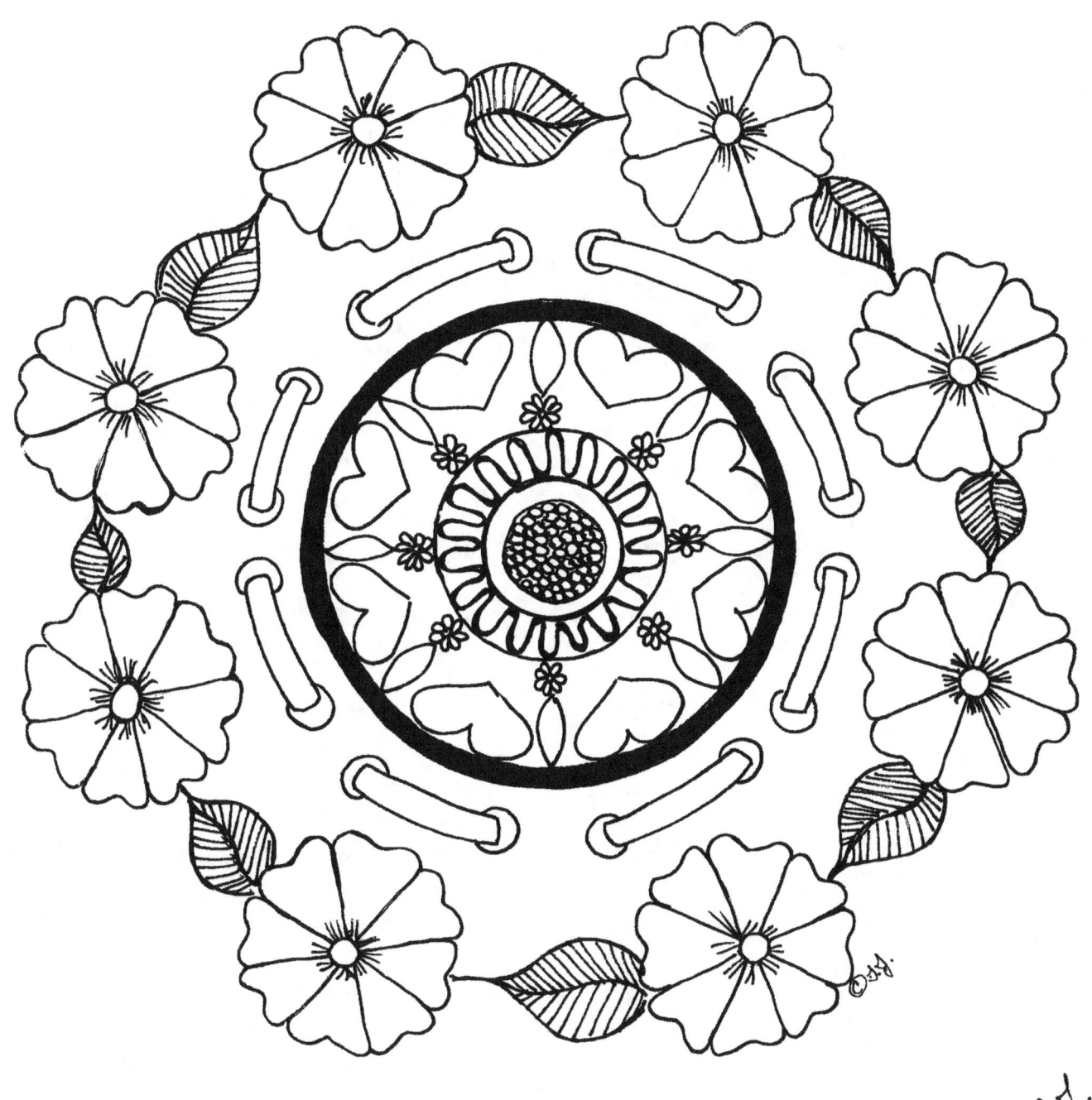

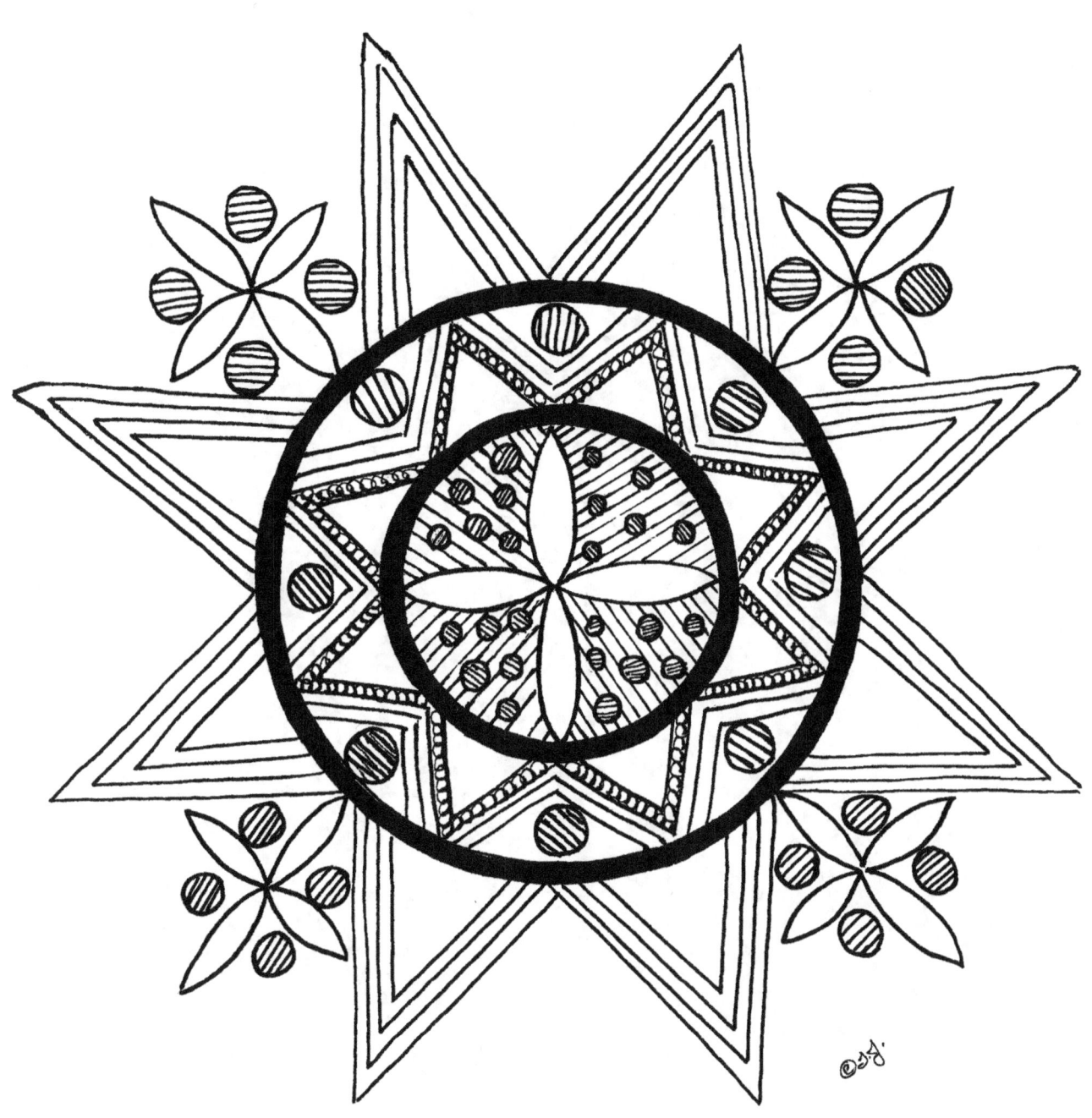

Contributing Artist
Pica Wu
Taiwan

Facebook : picapicadrow2

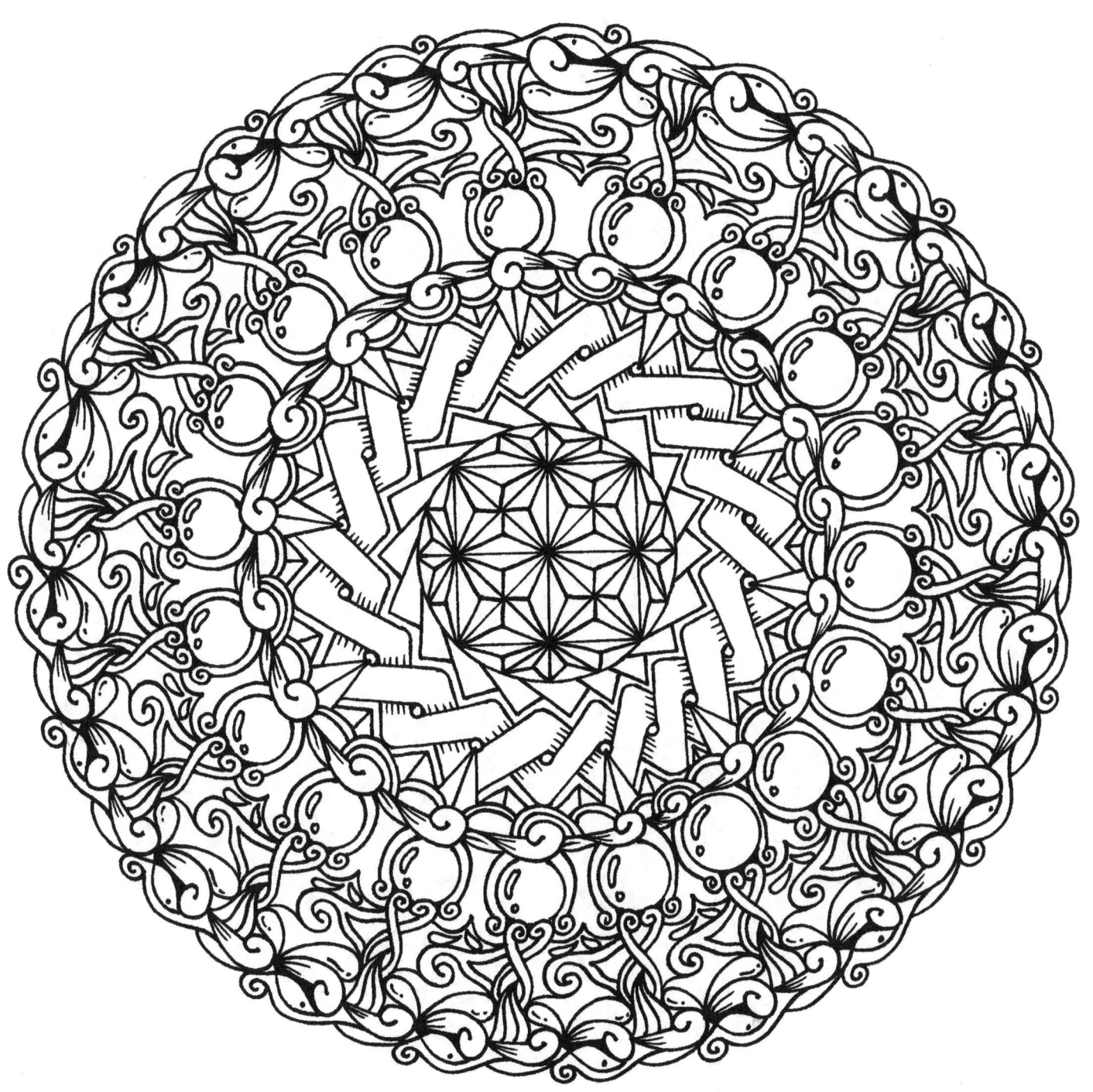

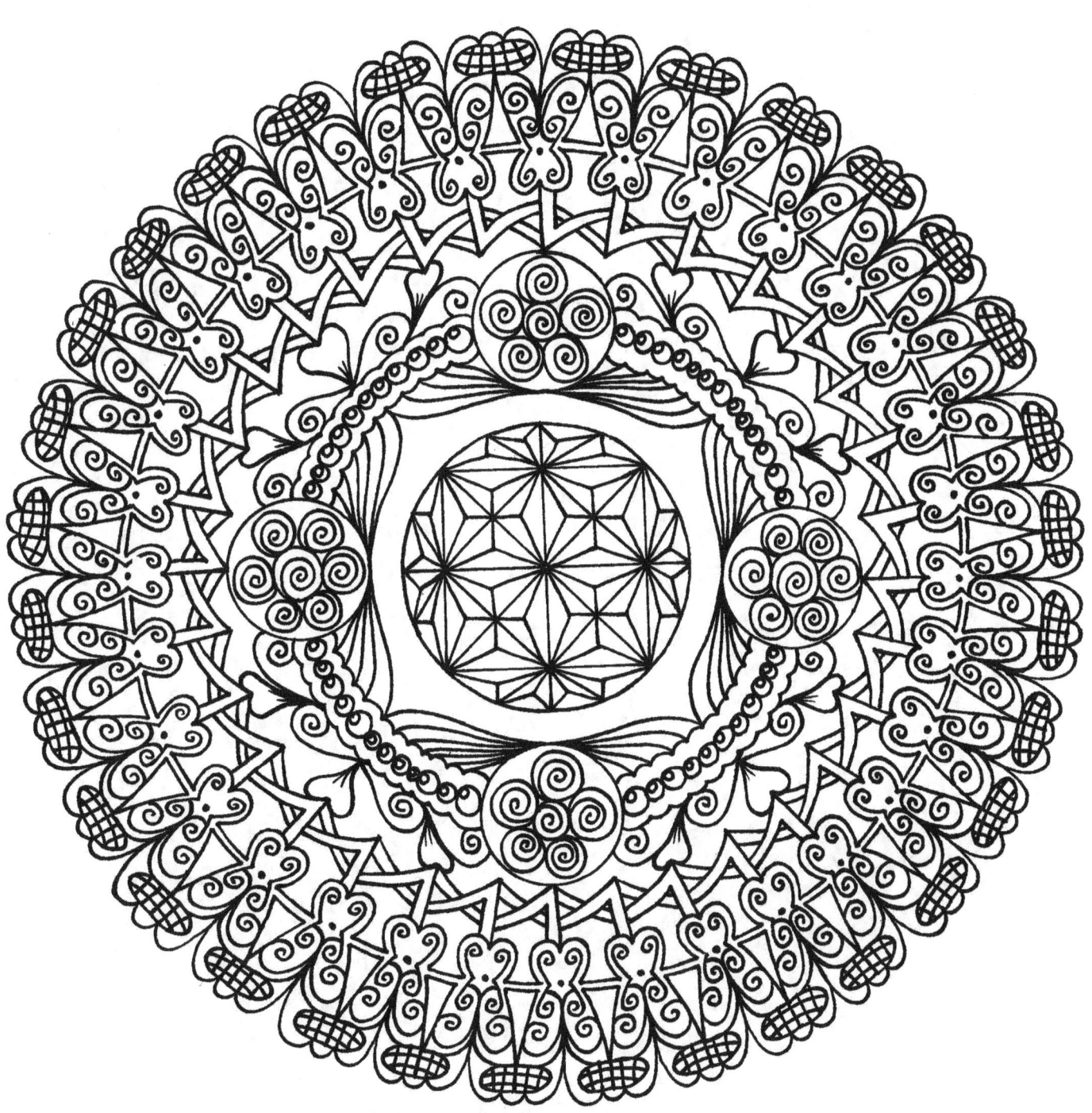

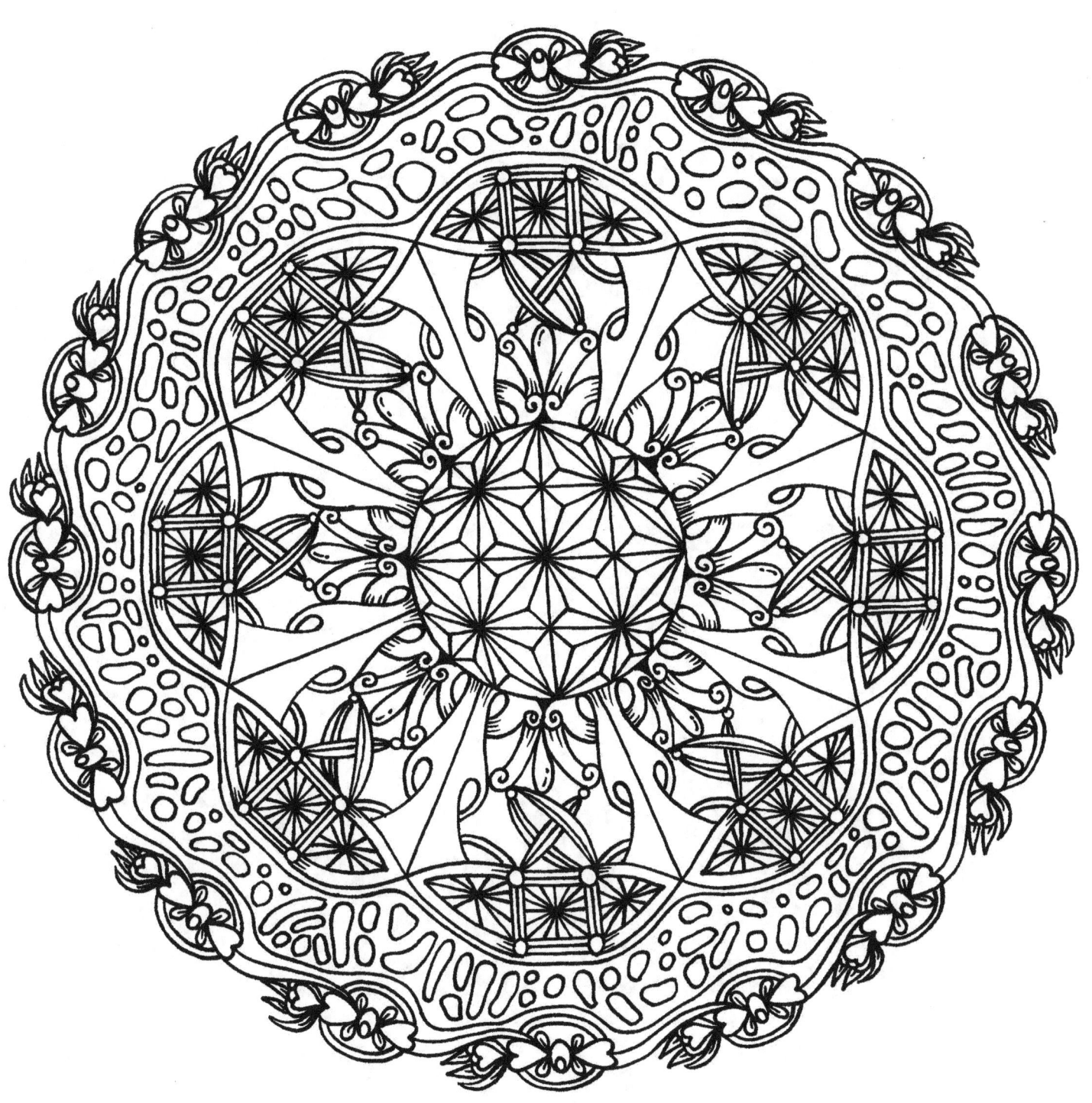

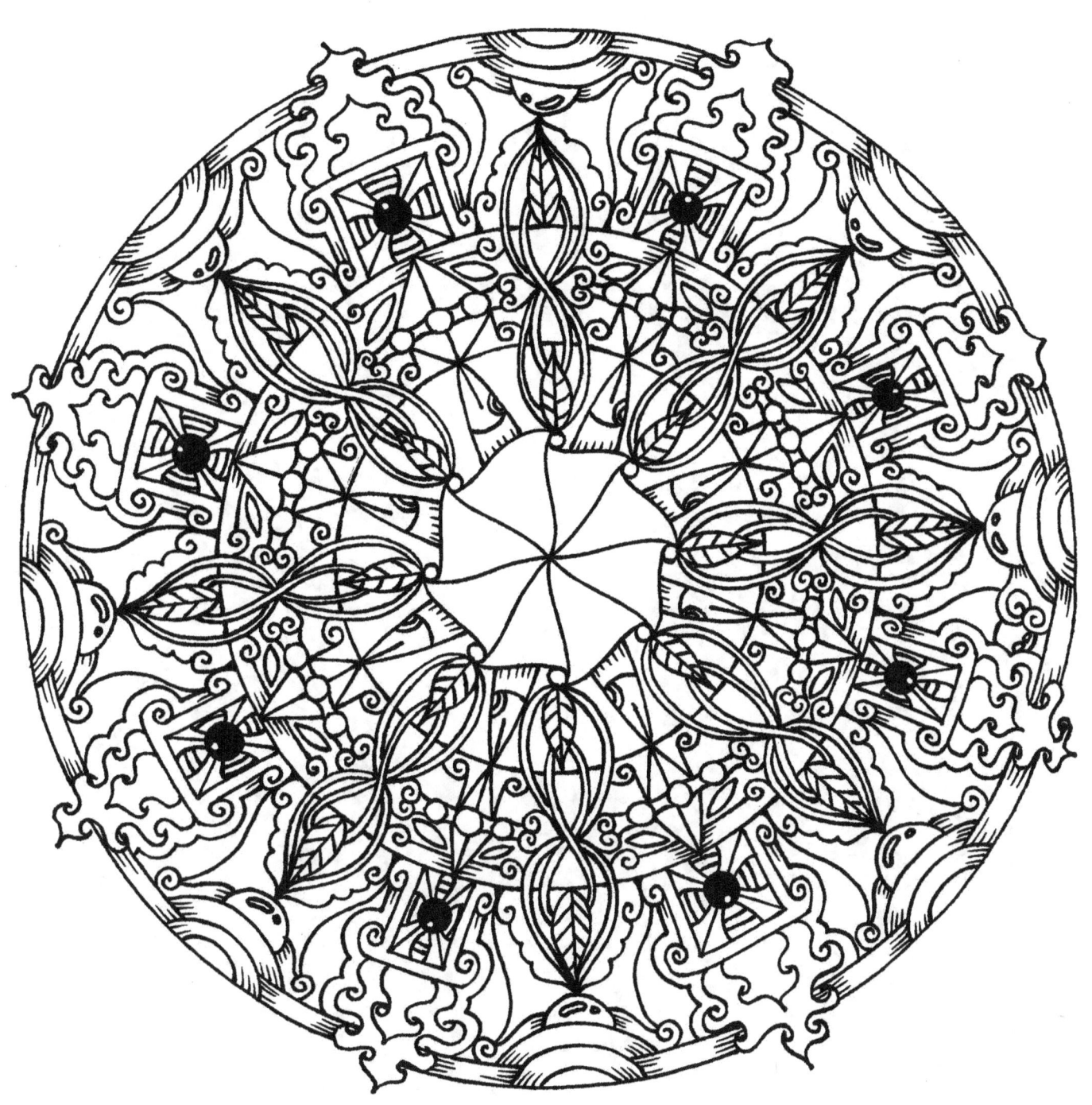

Contributing Artist
Ahmed Fouad Eid
Egypt
Facebook : Celestialarttherapy

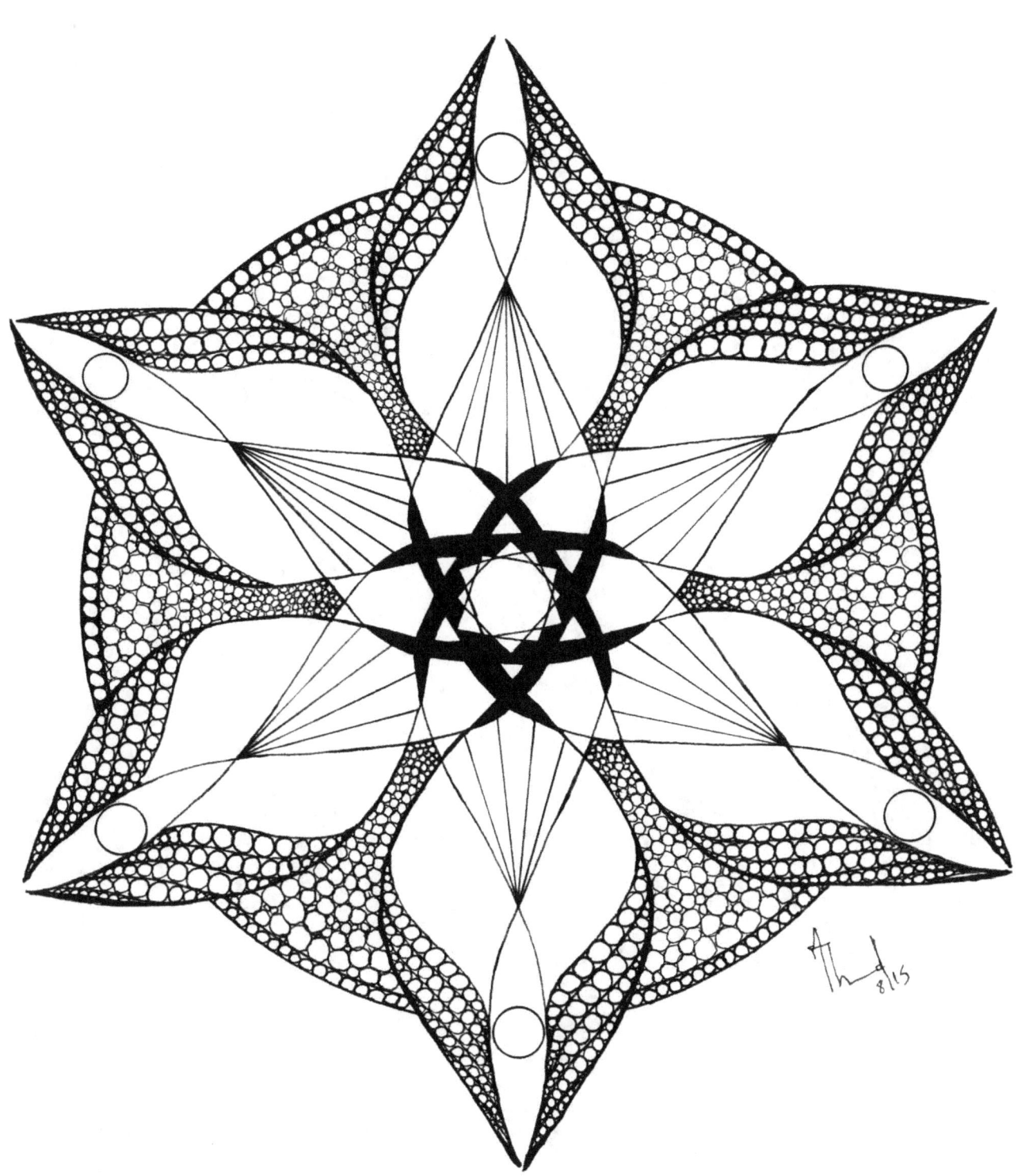

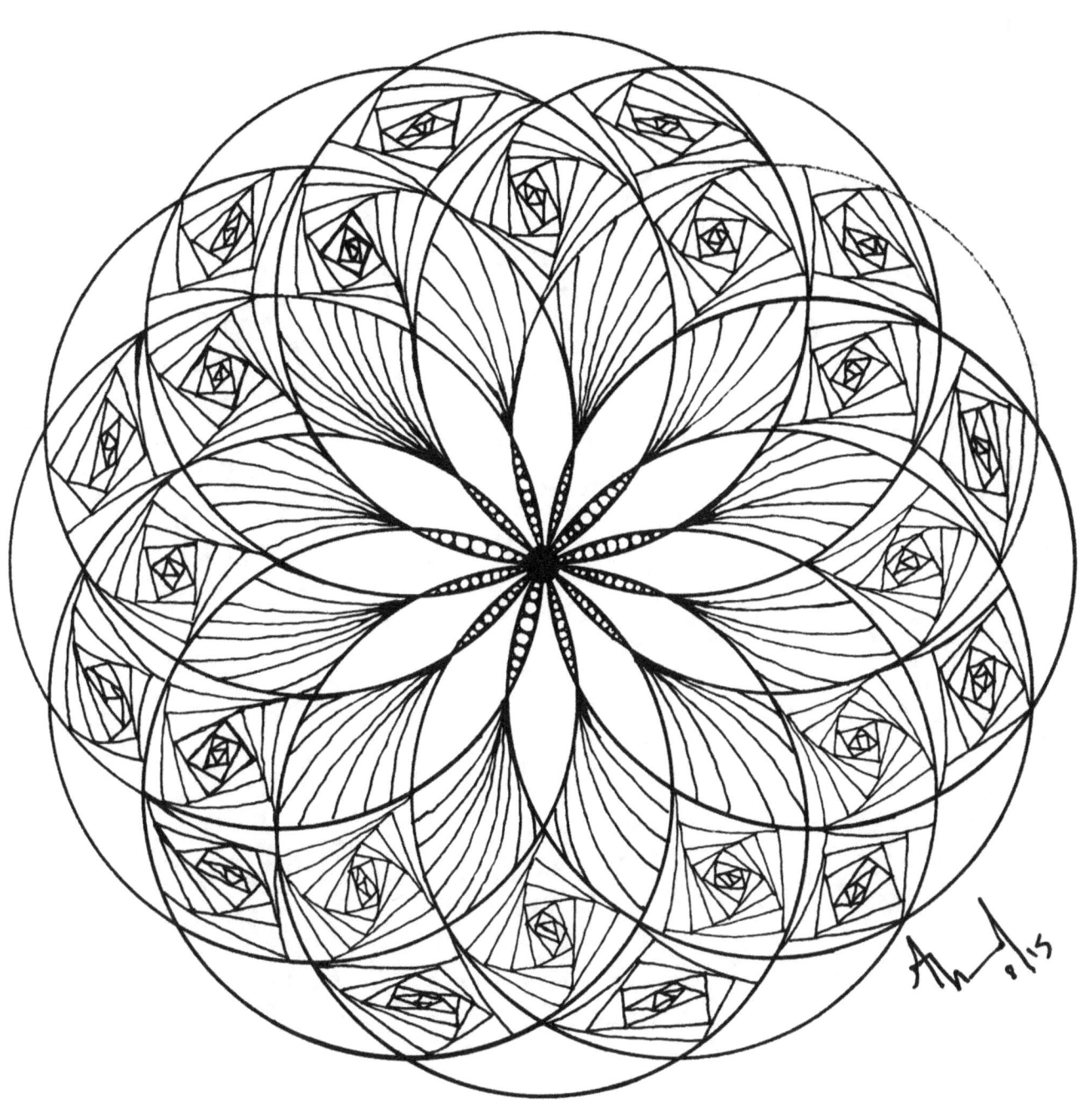

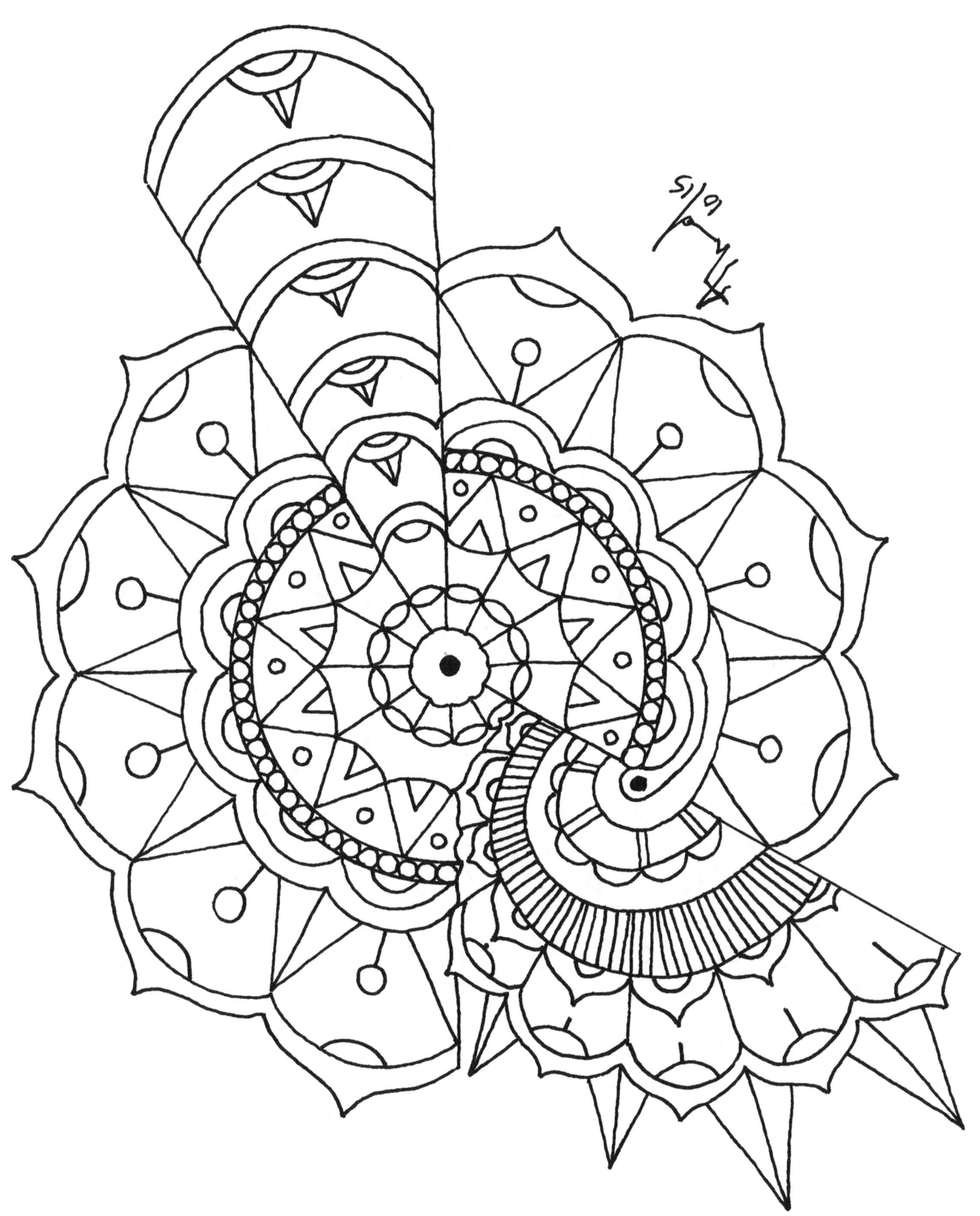

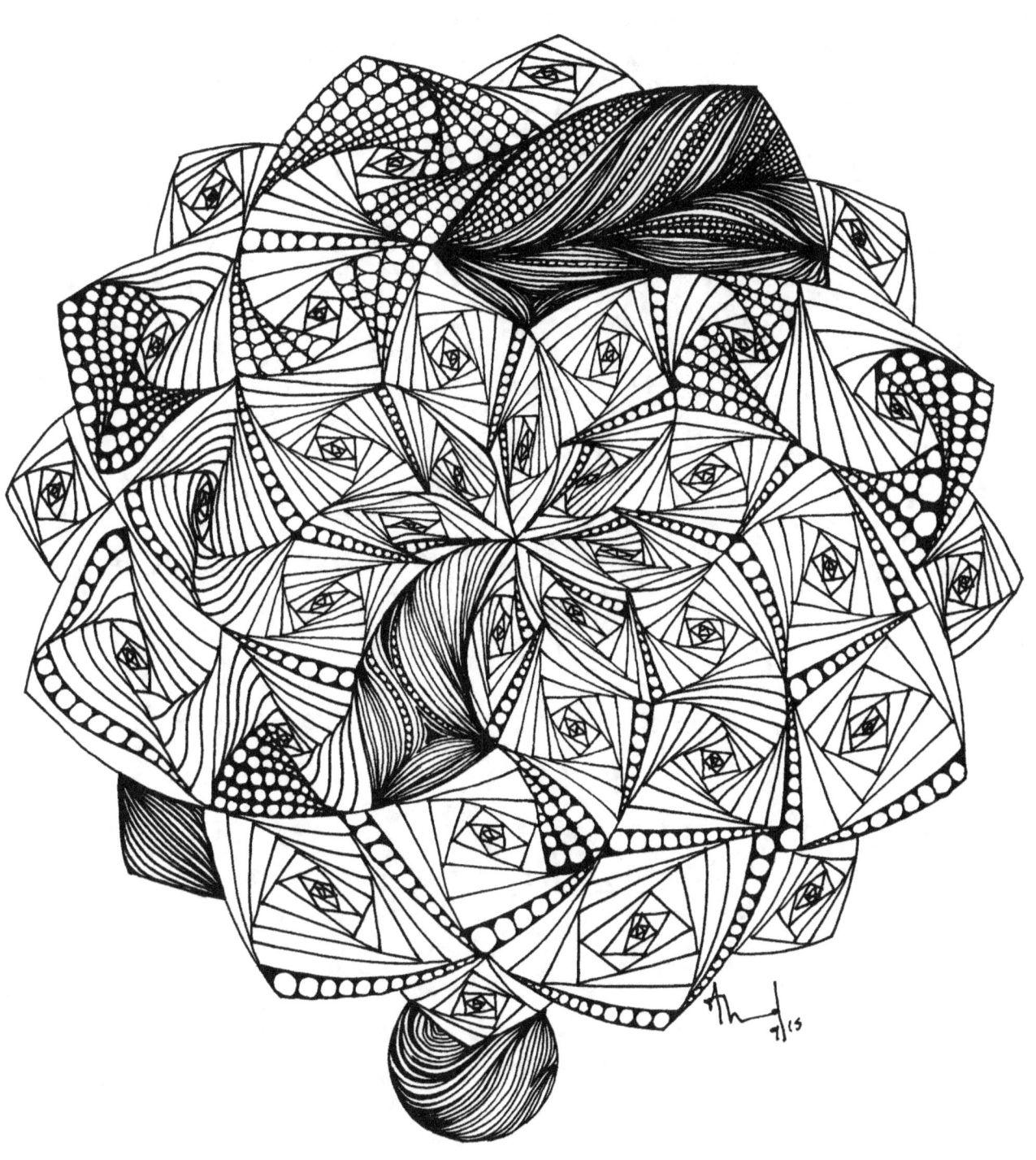

Contributing Artist
Rover Hsiao
Taiwan

Facebook : roverhsiao2015

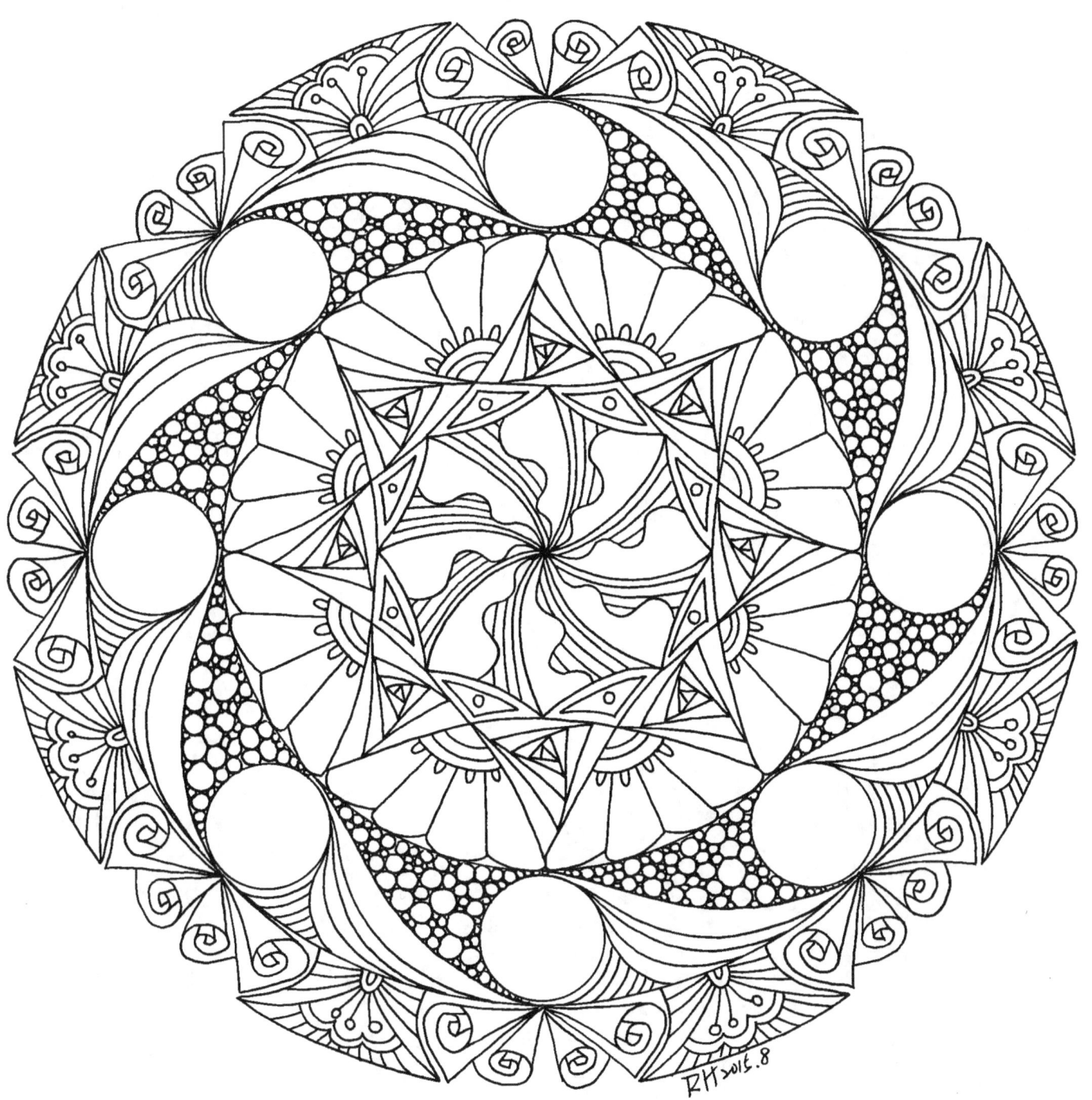

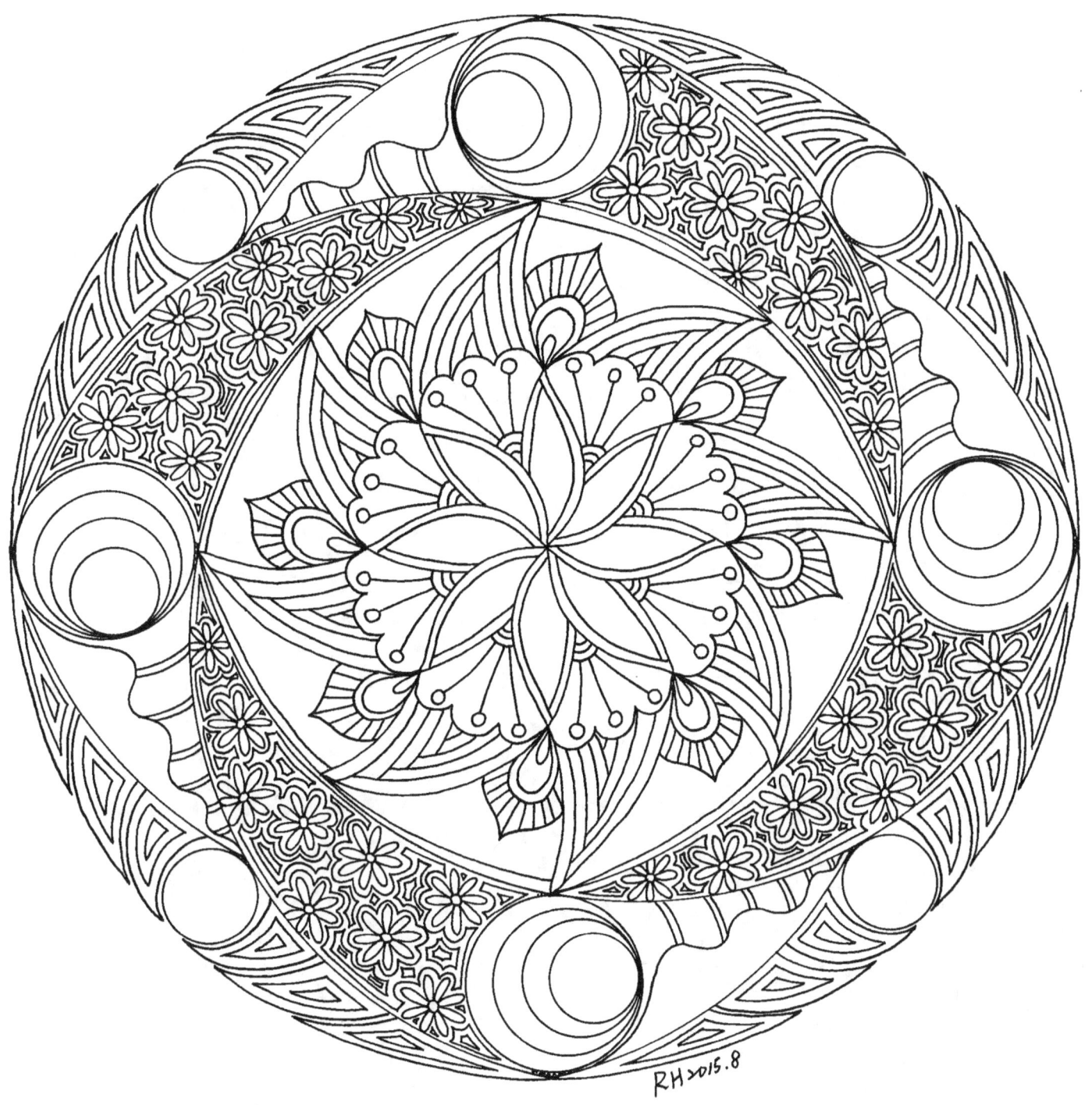

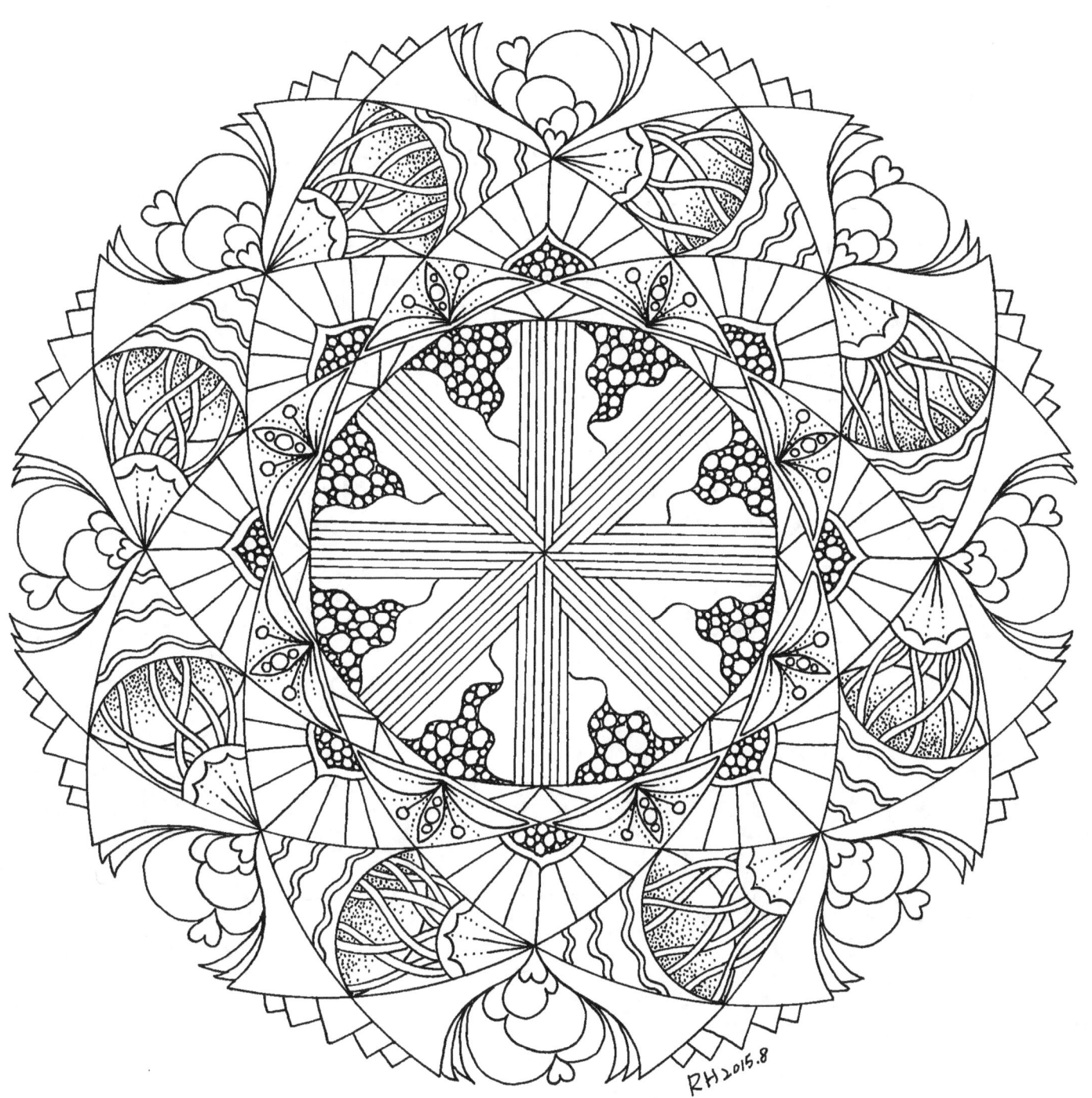

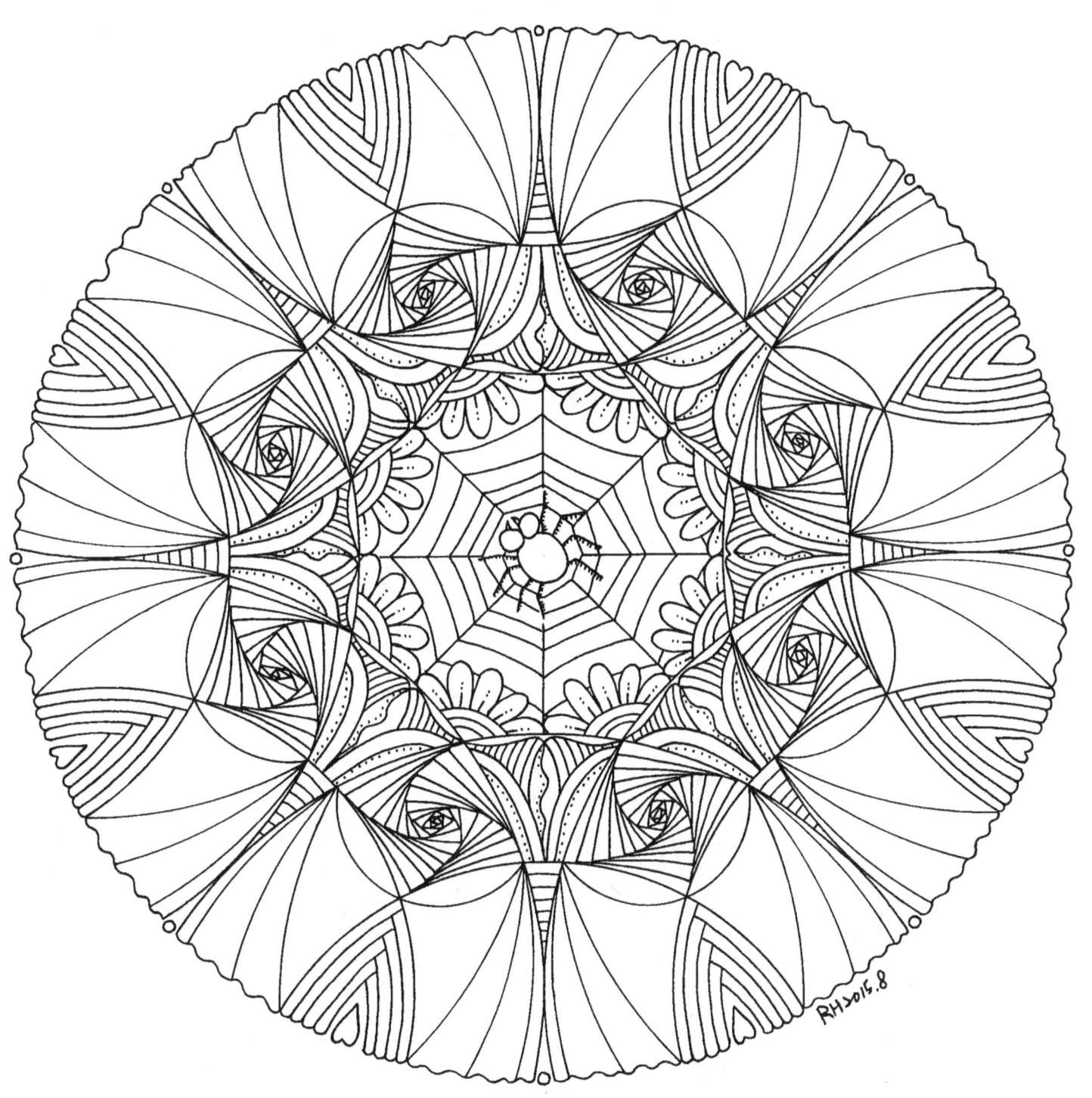

Contributing Artist
Yaya
France

Facebook : Les-gribouillis-de-yaya-georgia-merino

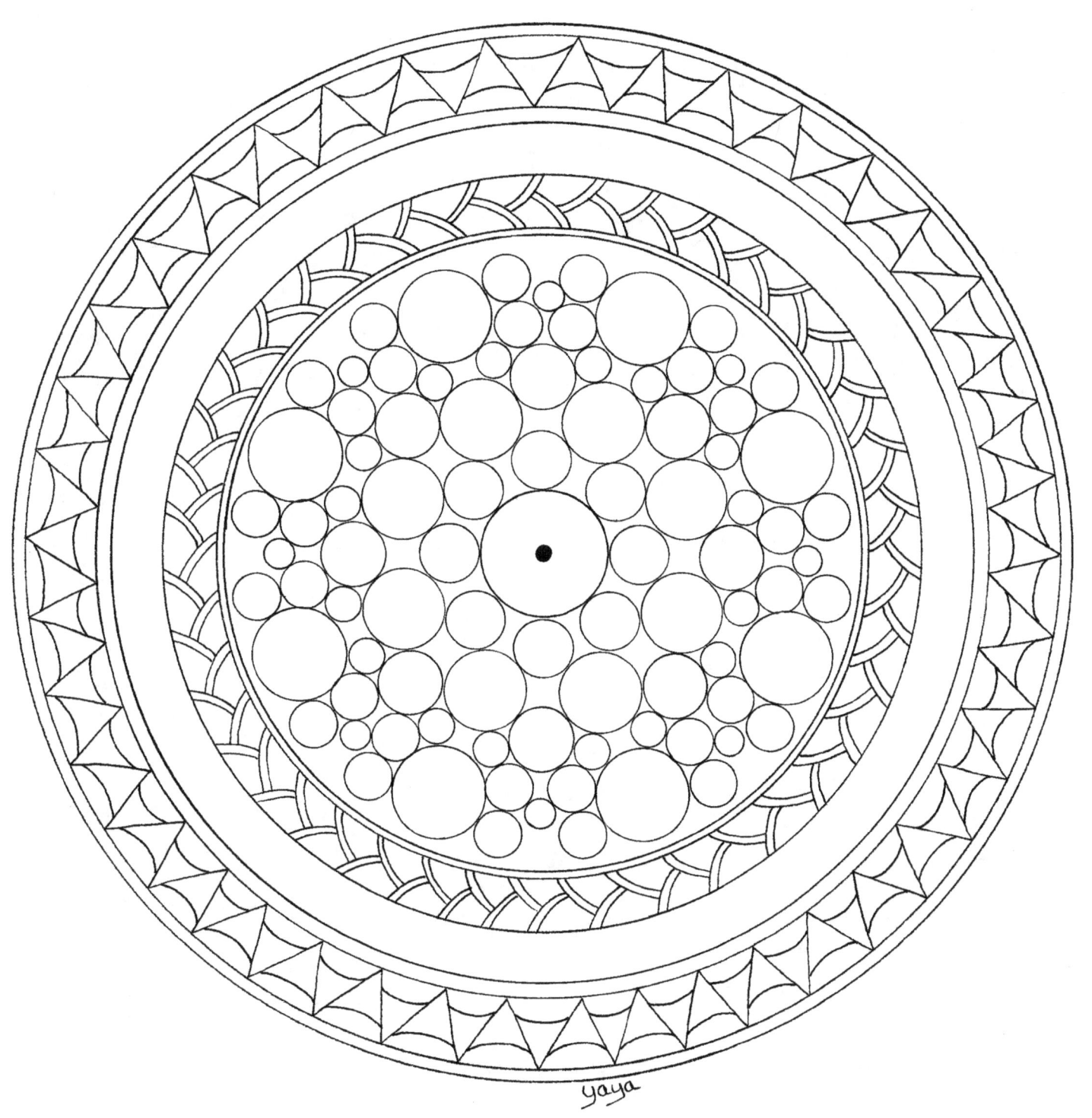

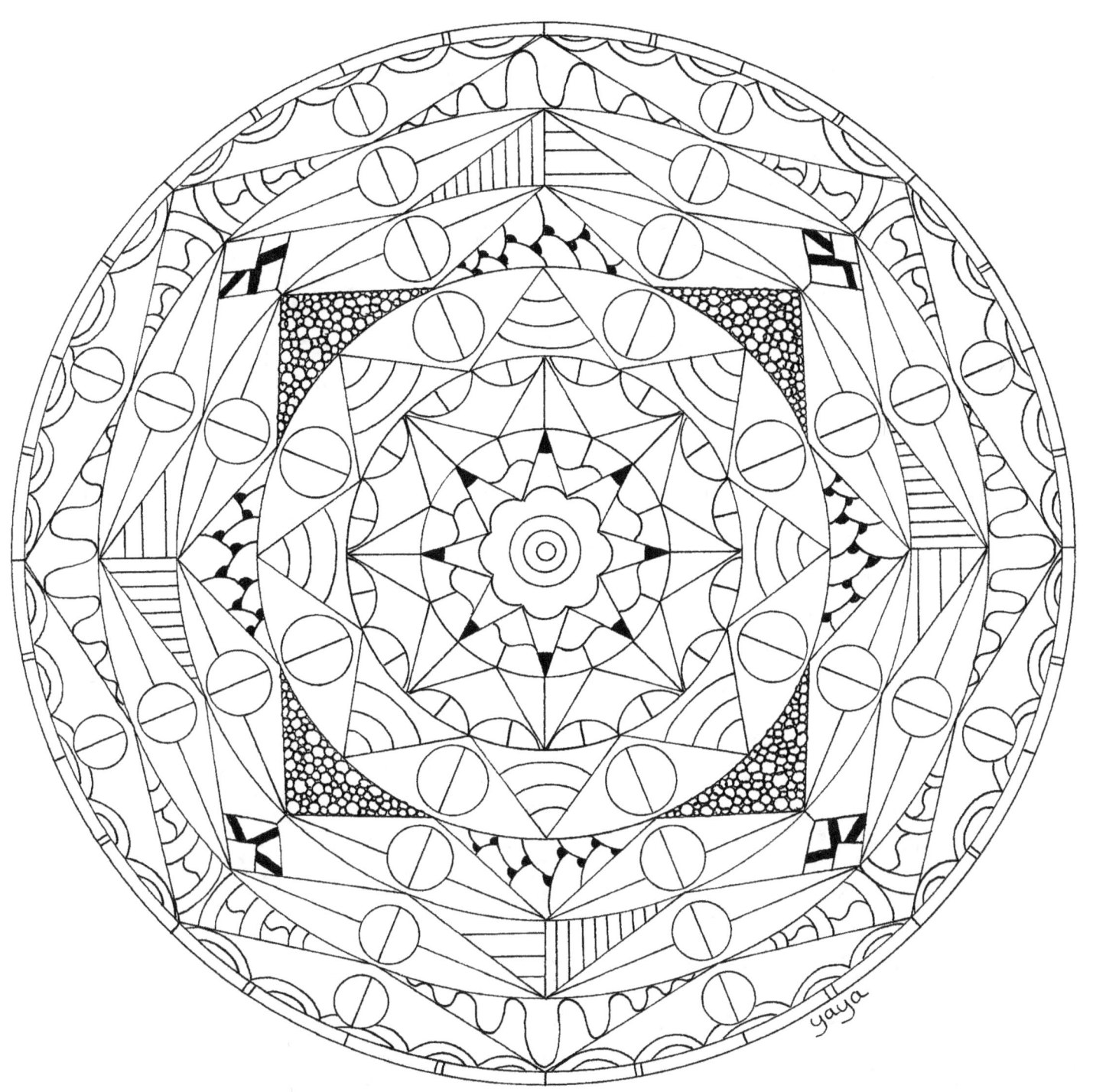

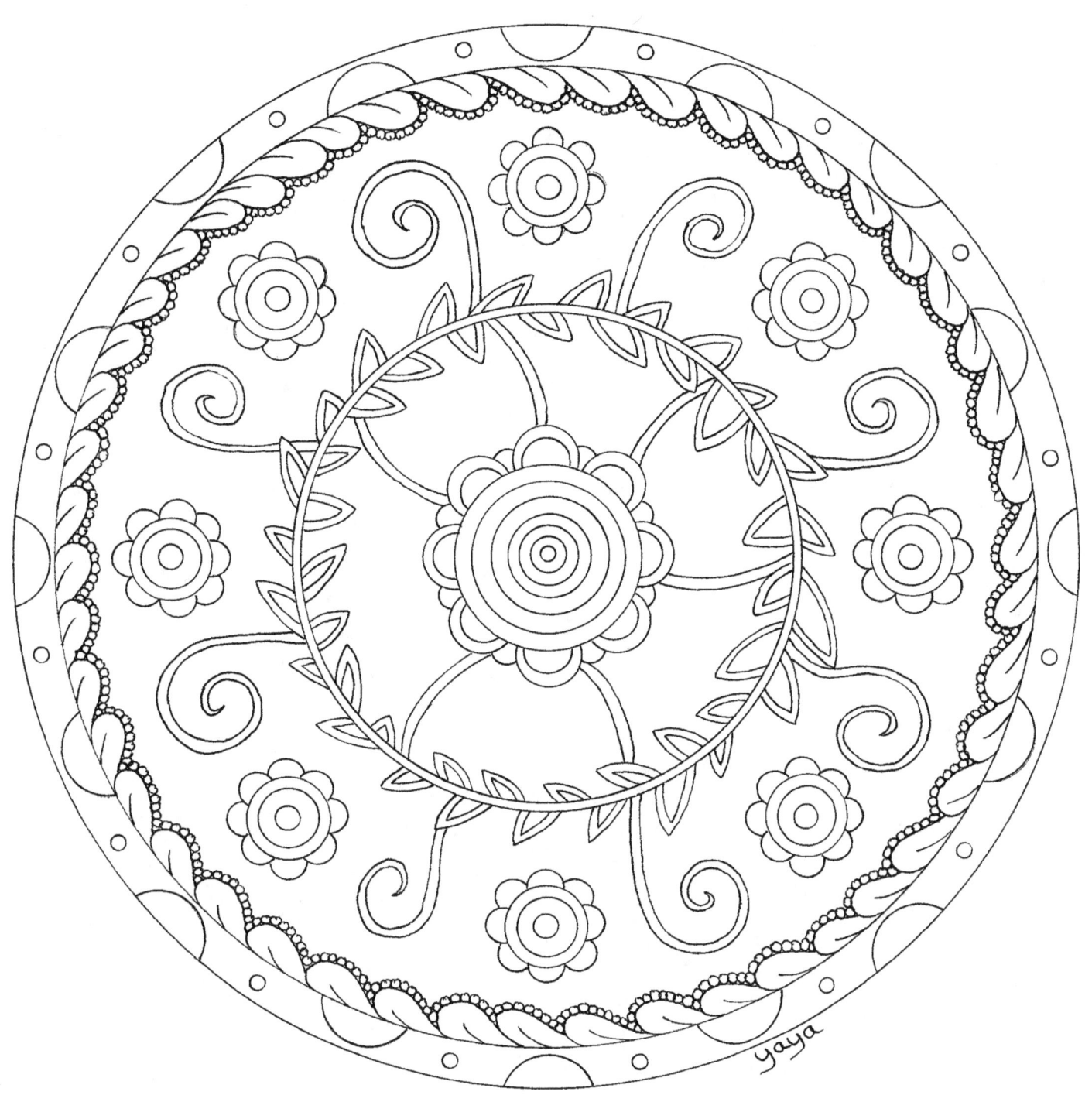

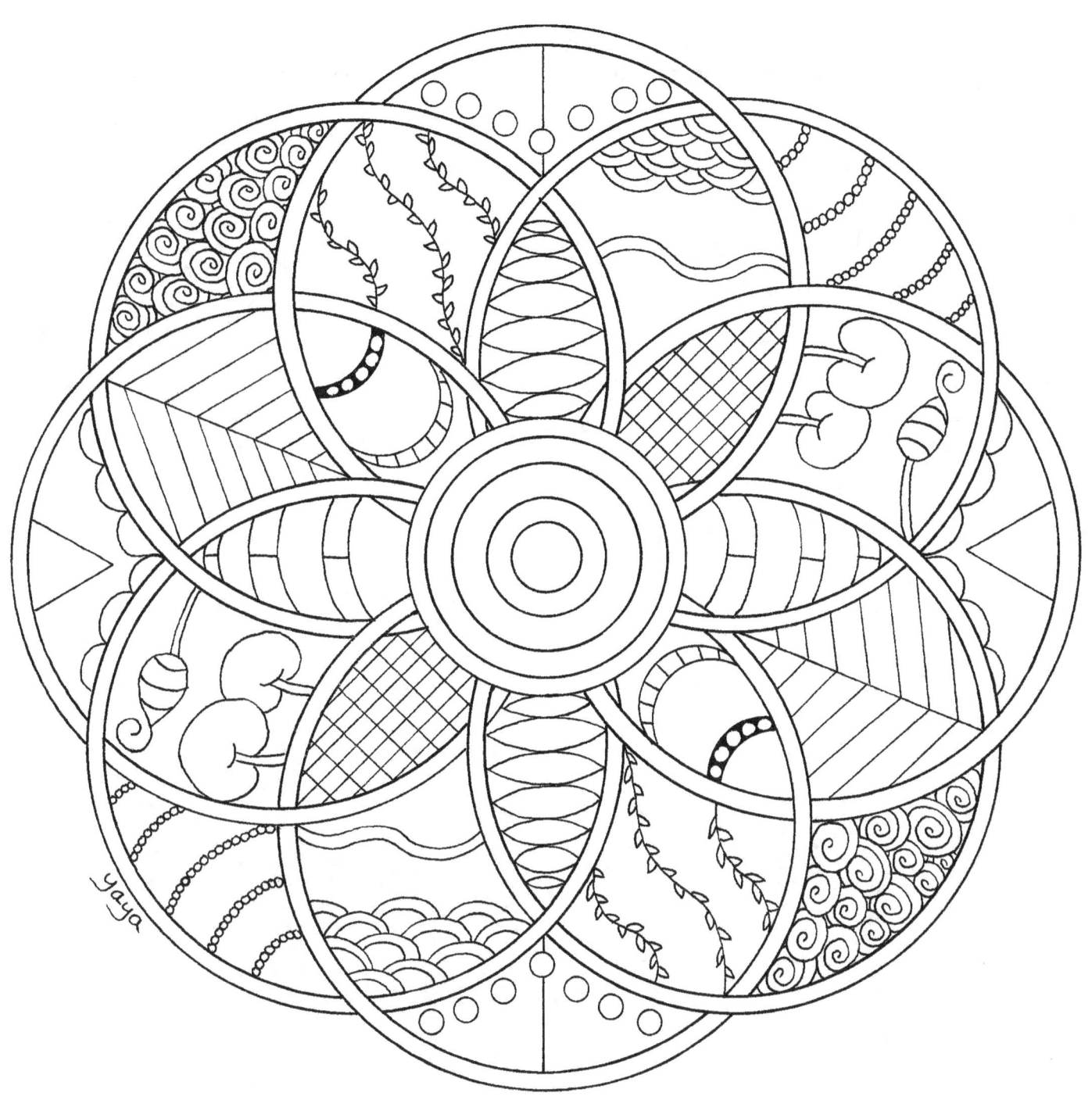

Contributing Artist

Marieke Raterman-Bos
Monnickendam, the Netherlands

www.monnickenwerken.nl
Facebook : Monnicken-Werken-by-Marieke-Raterman

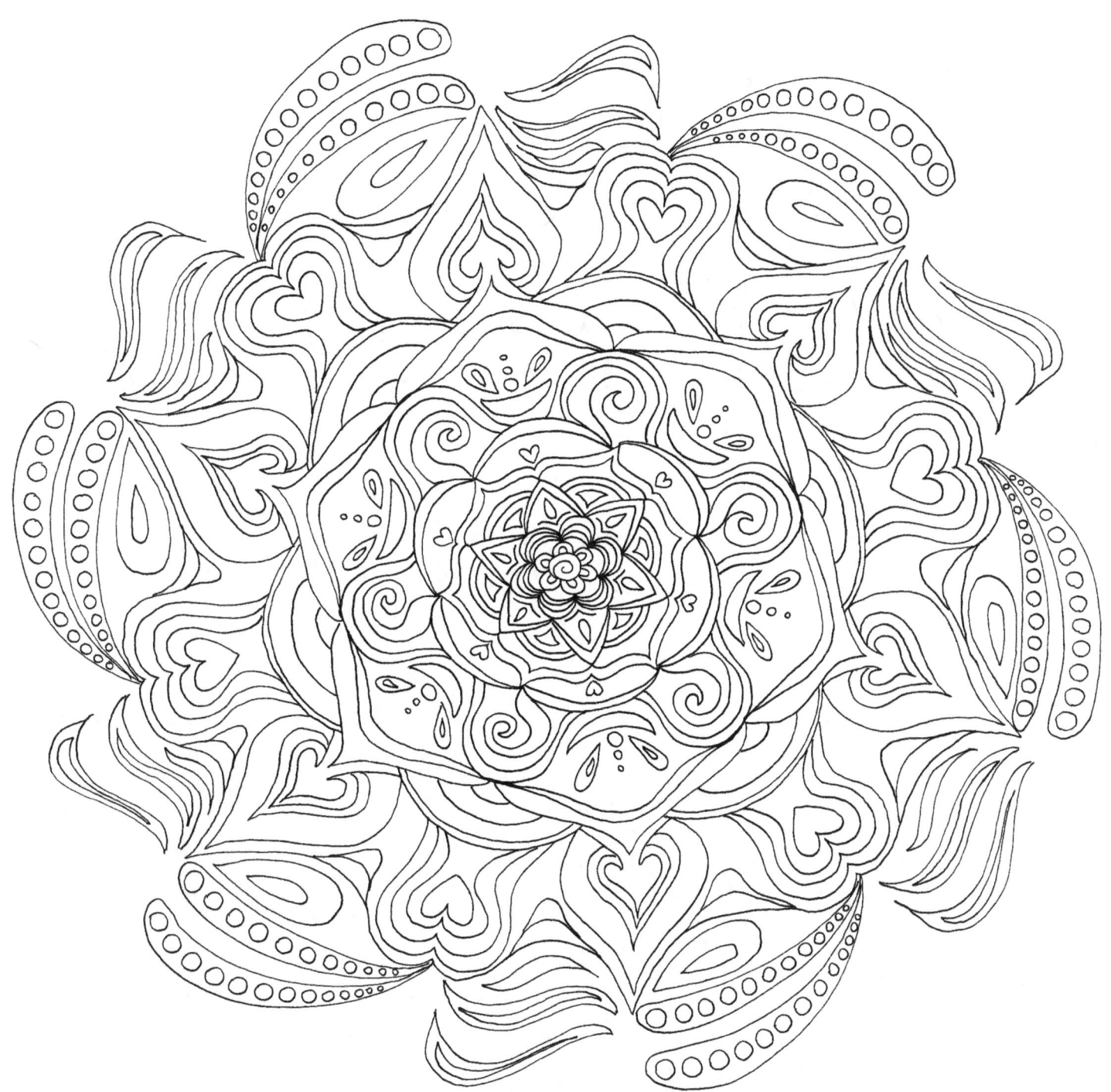

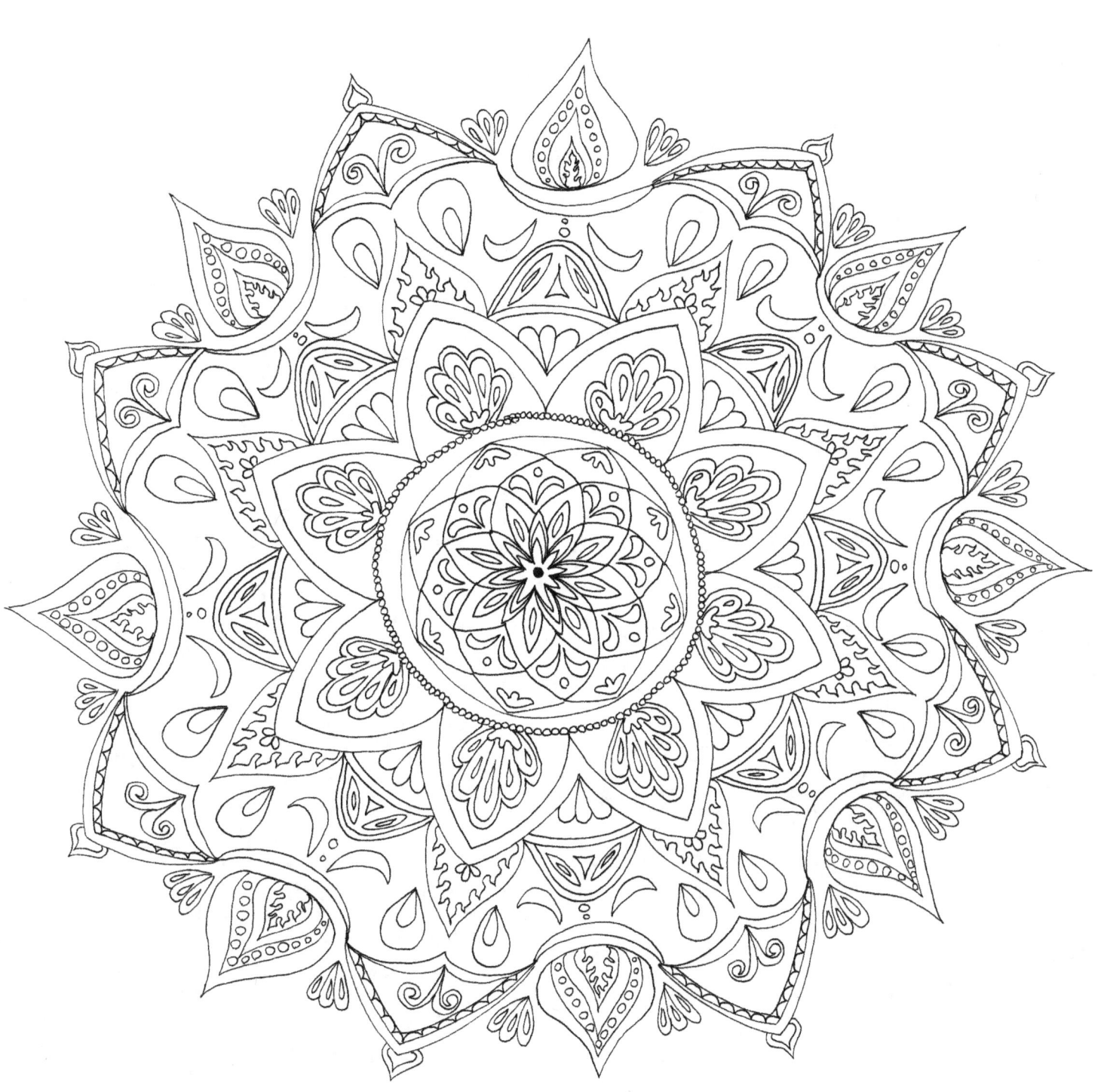

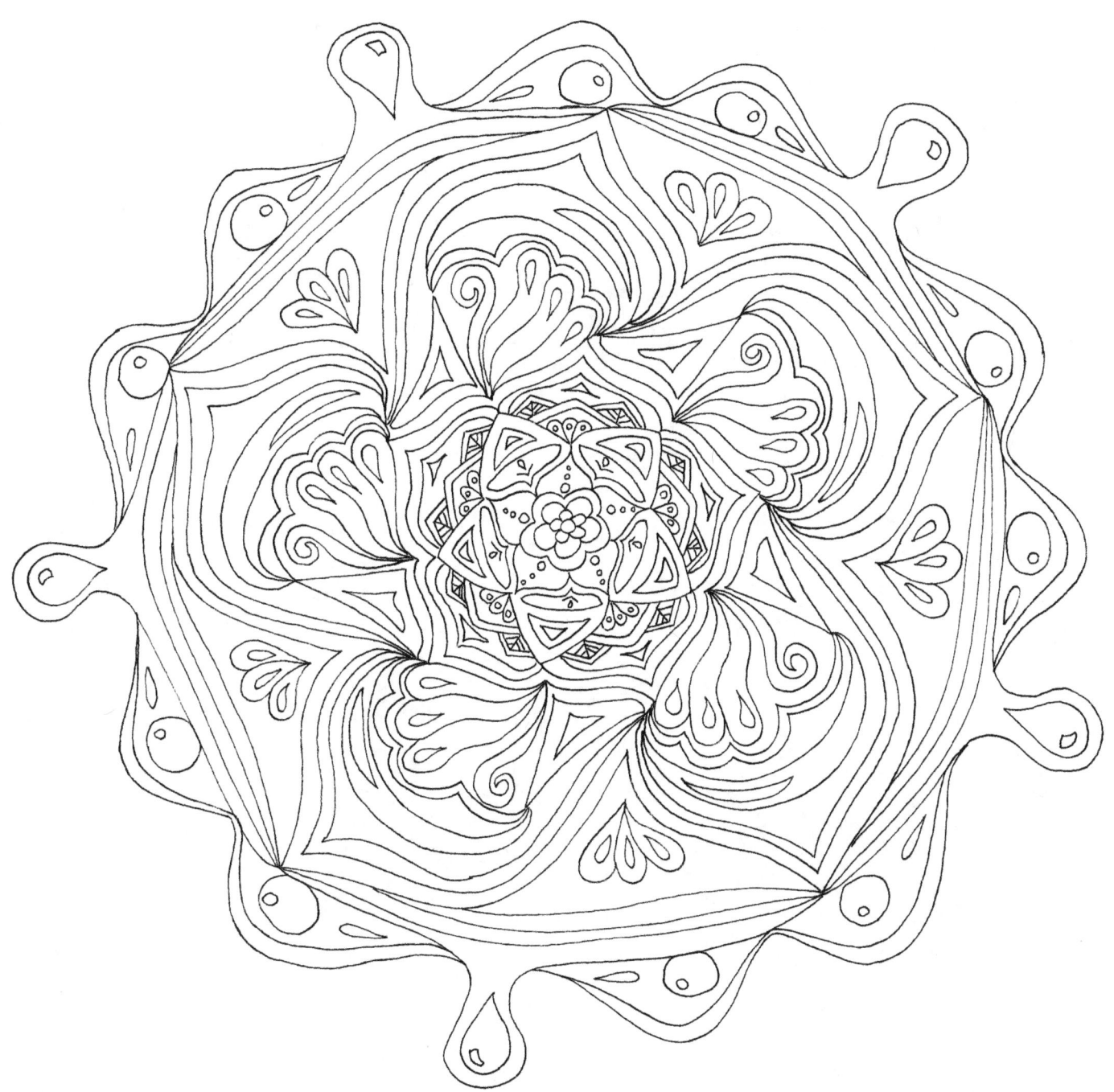

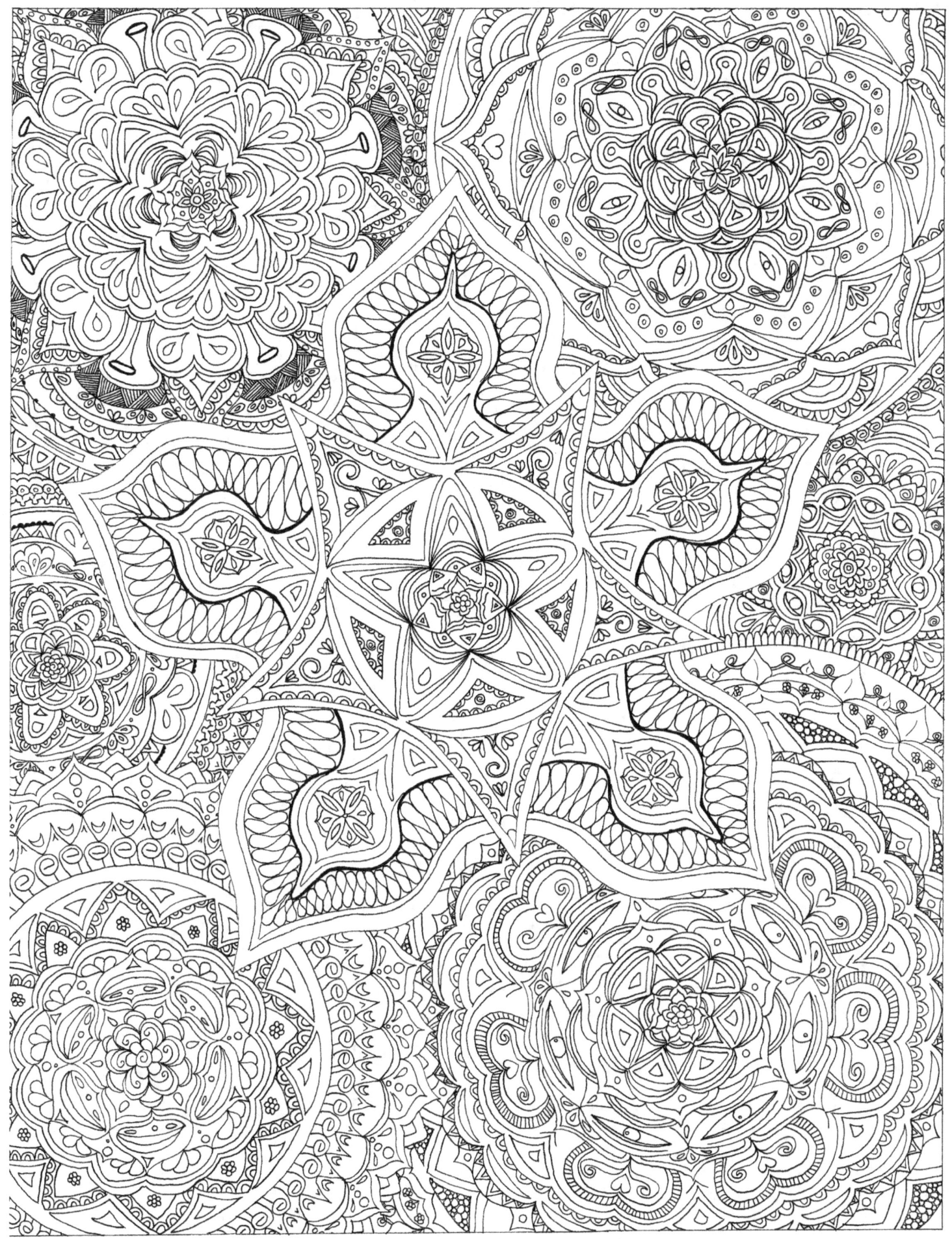

Contributing Artist
Dawn Miller
USA

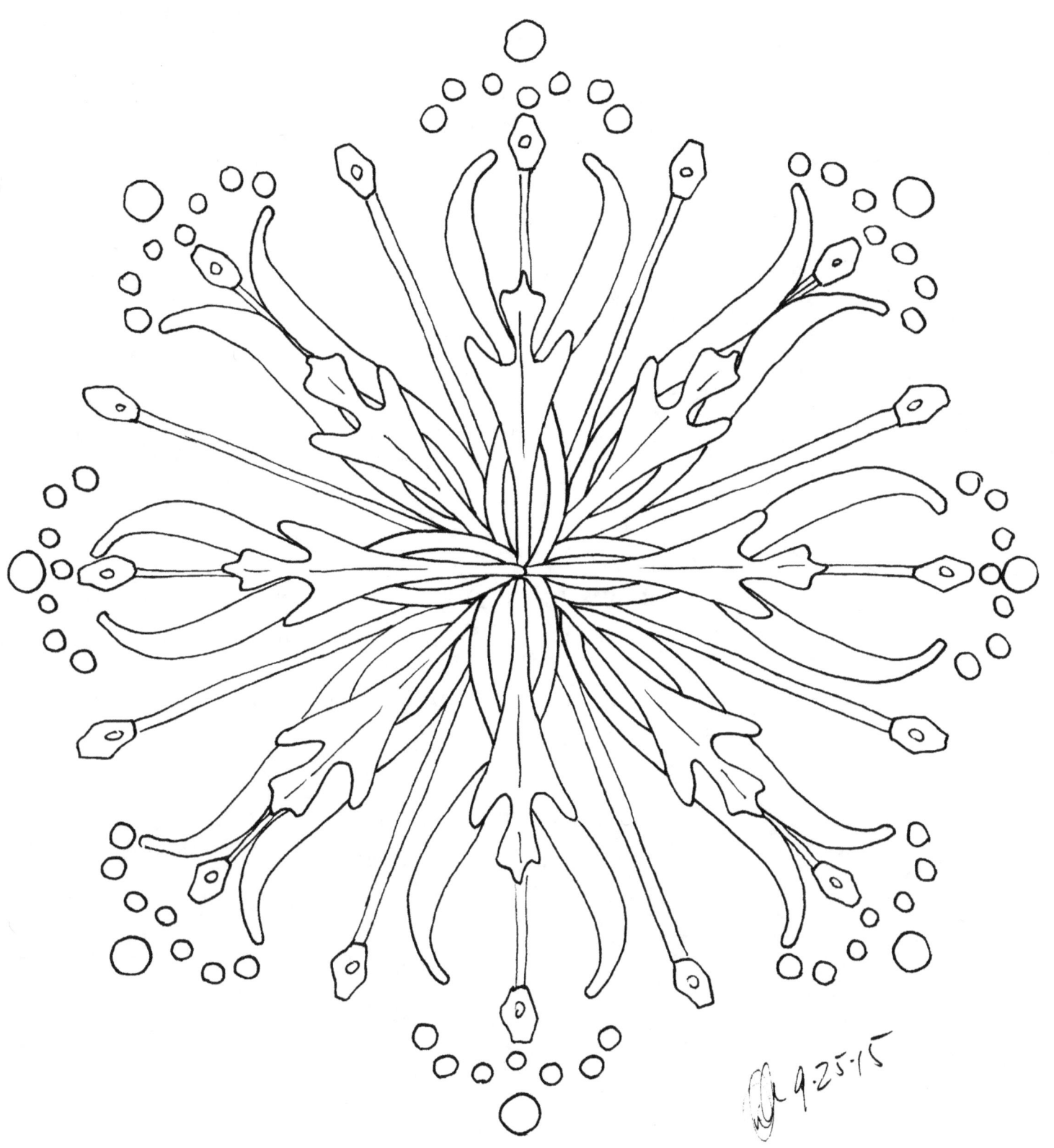

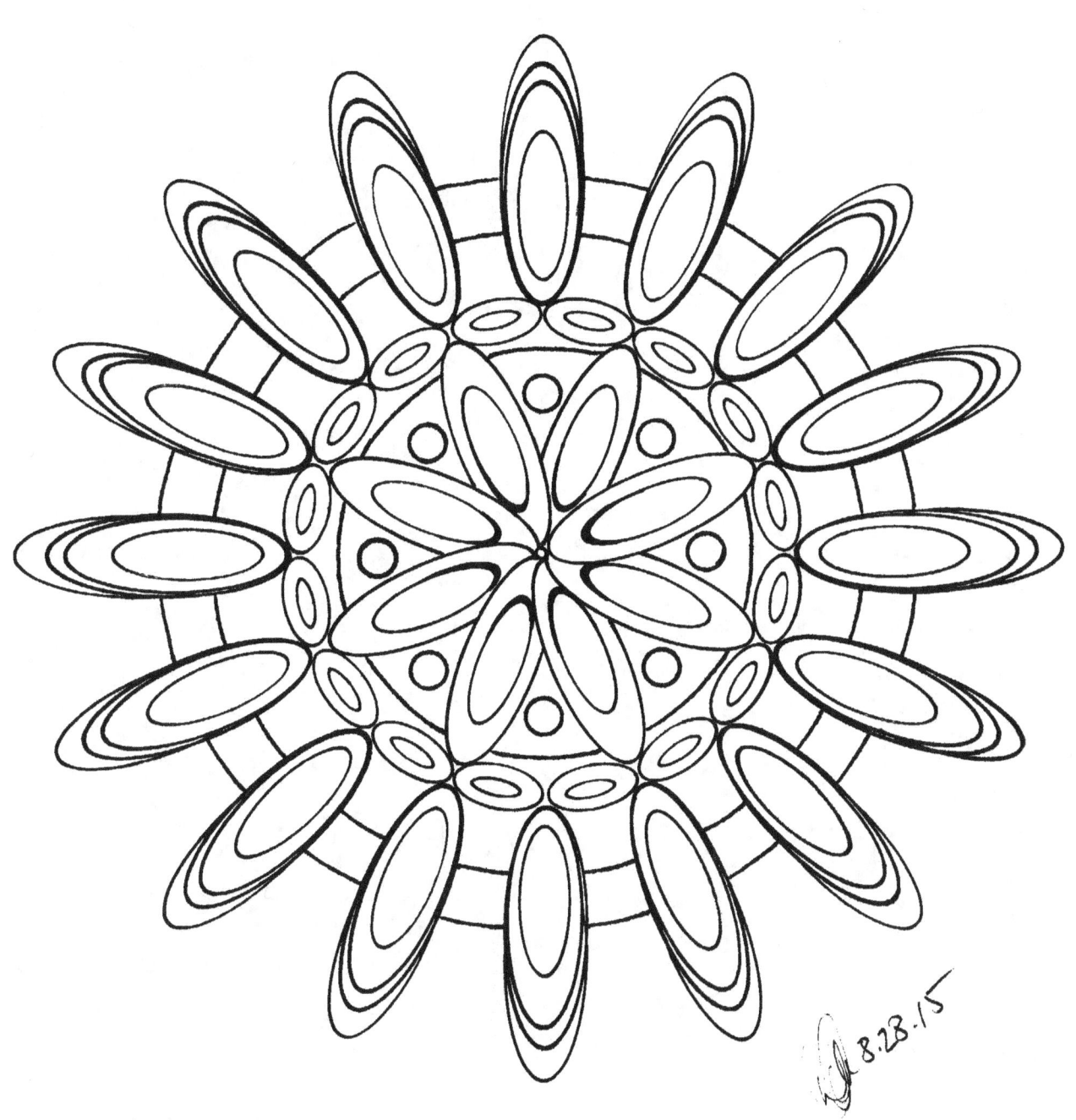

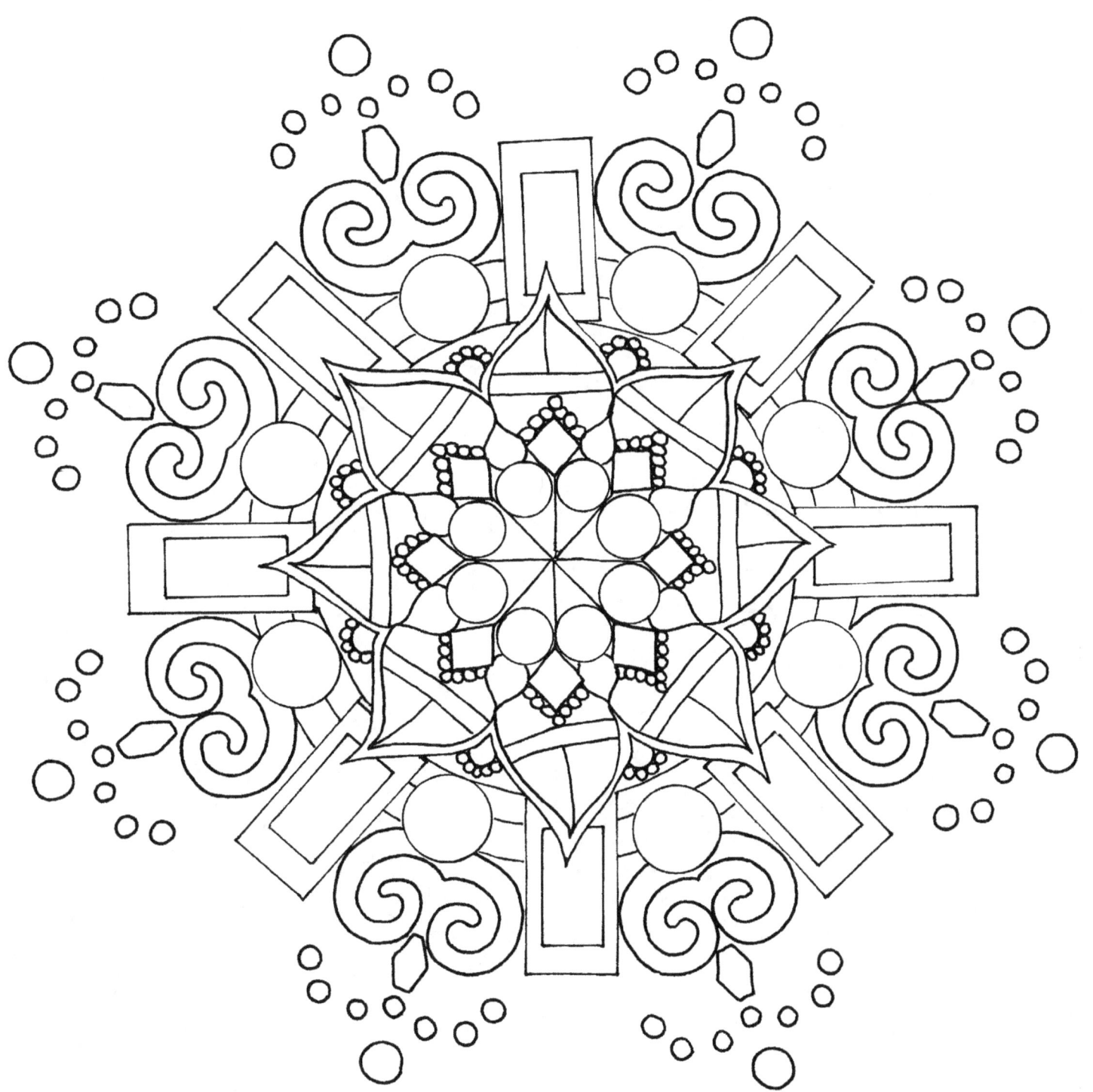

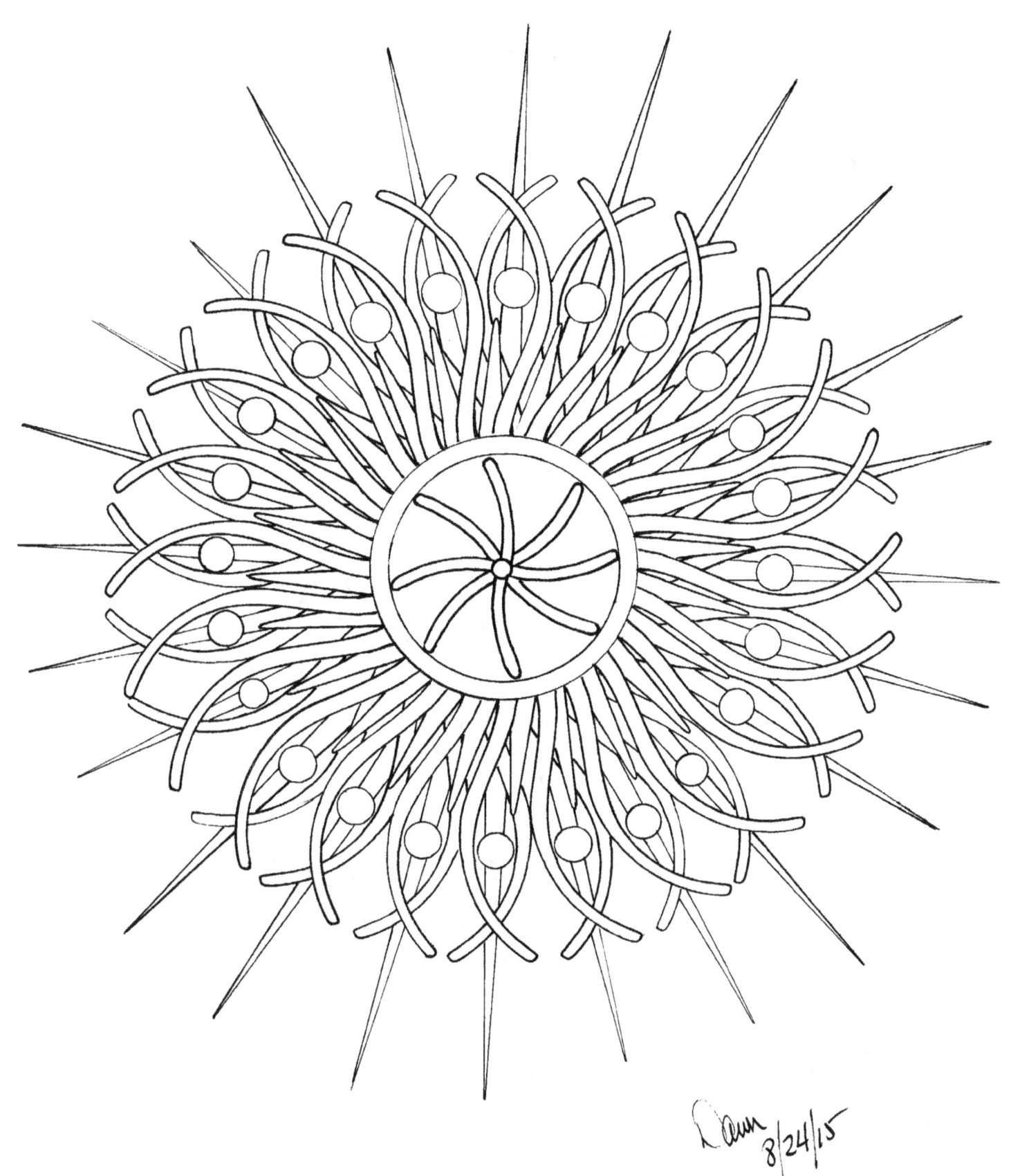

Contributing Artist
Audrey Sagh
Saskatoon, Saskatchewan Canada

Facebook : AMS-Artwork

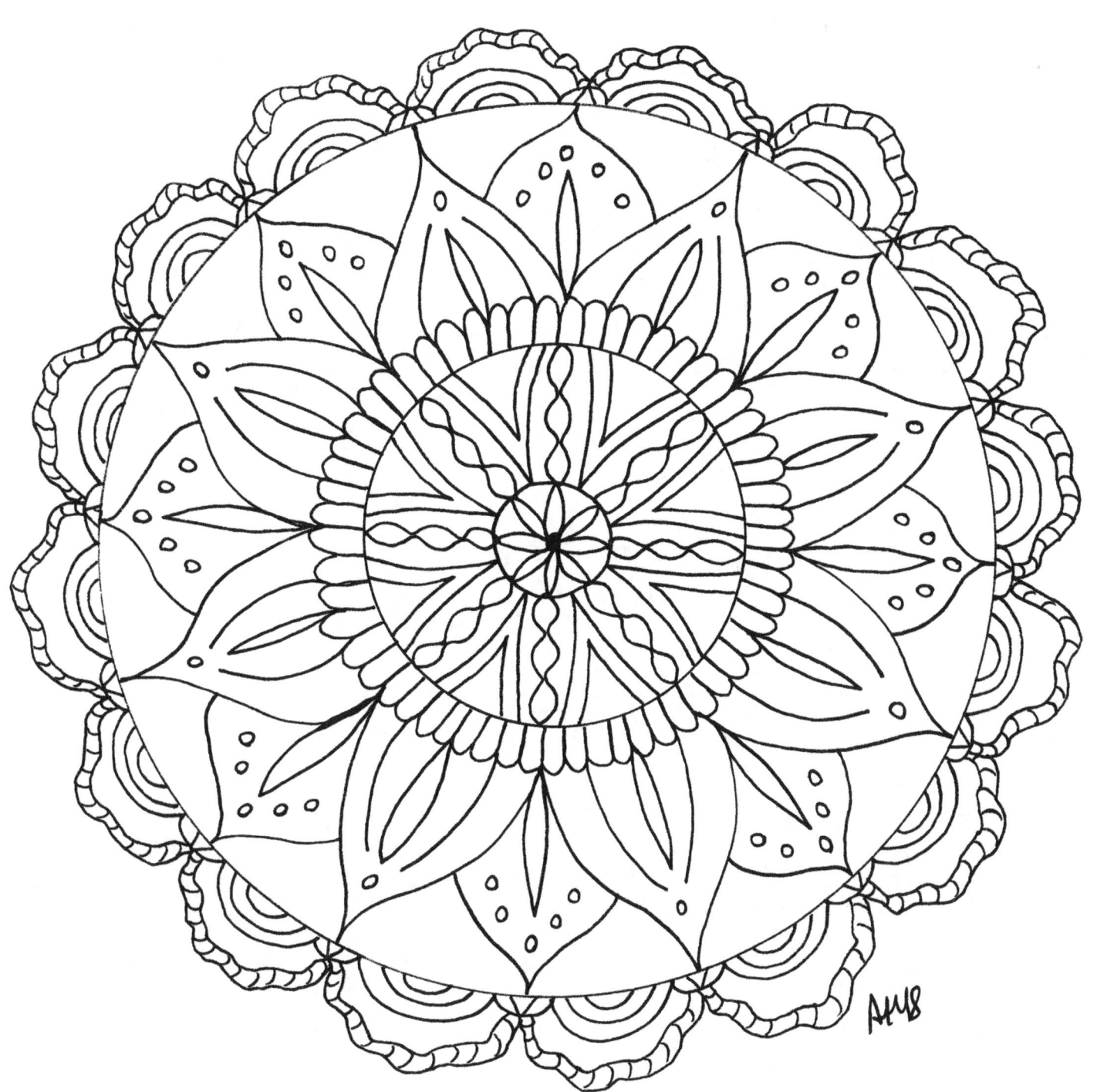

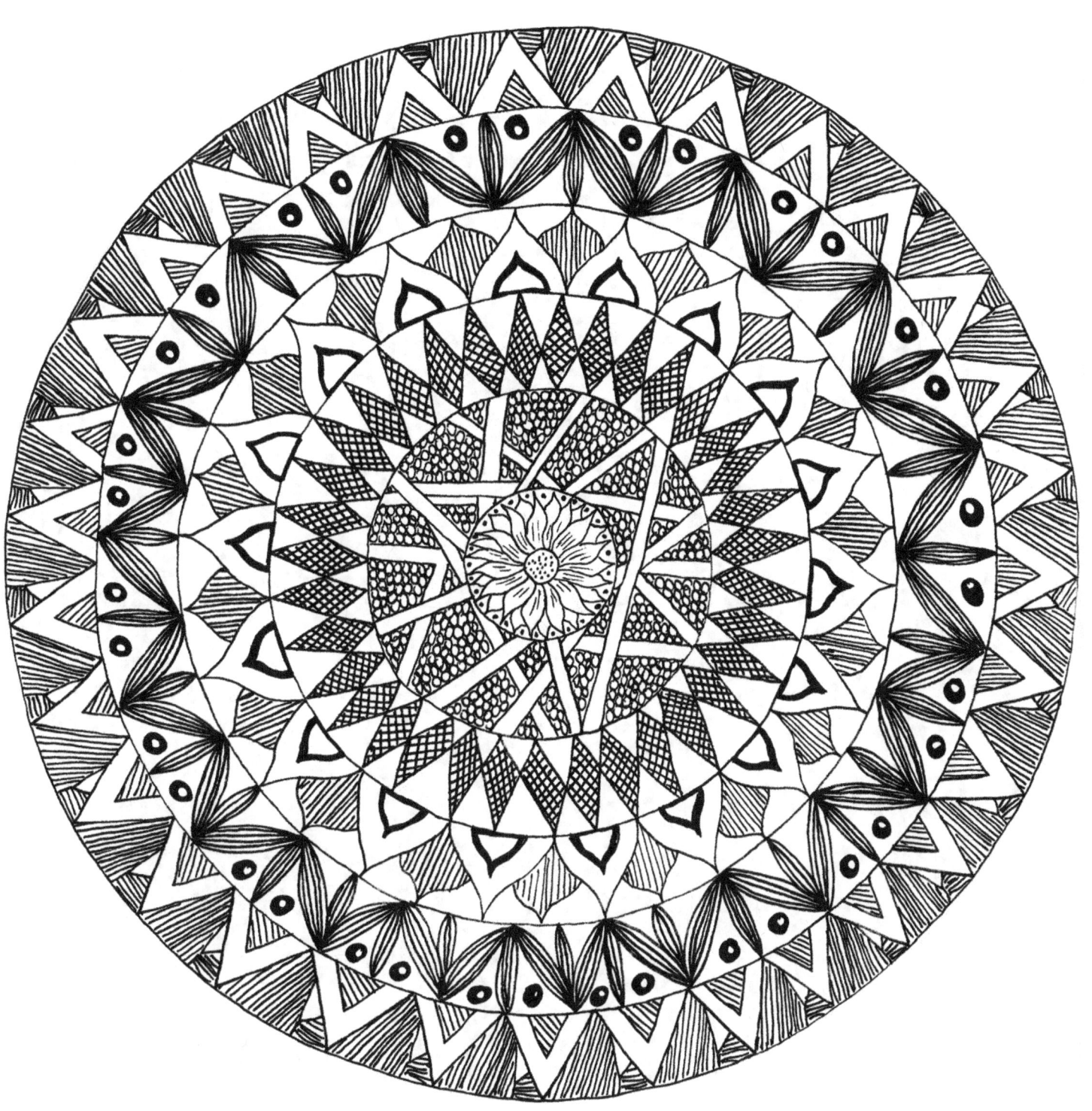

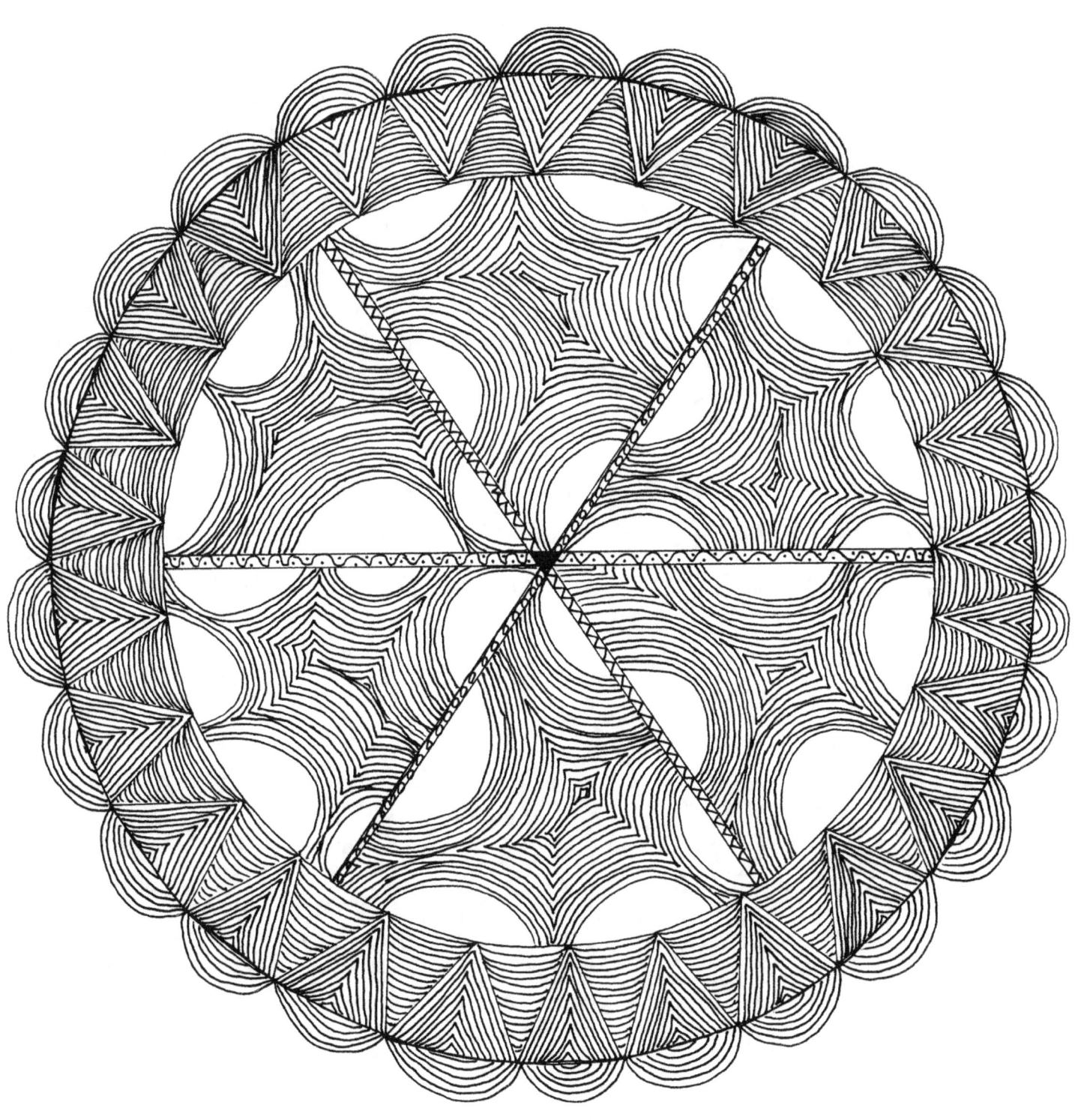

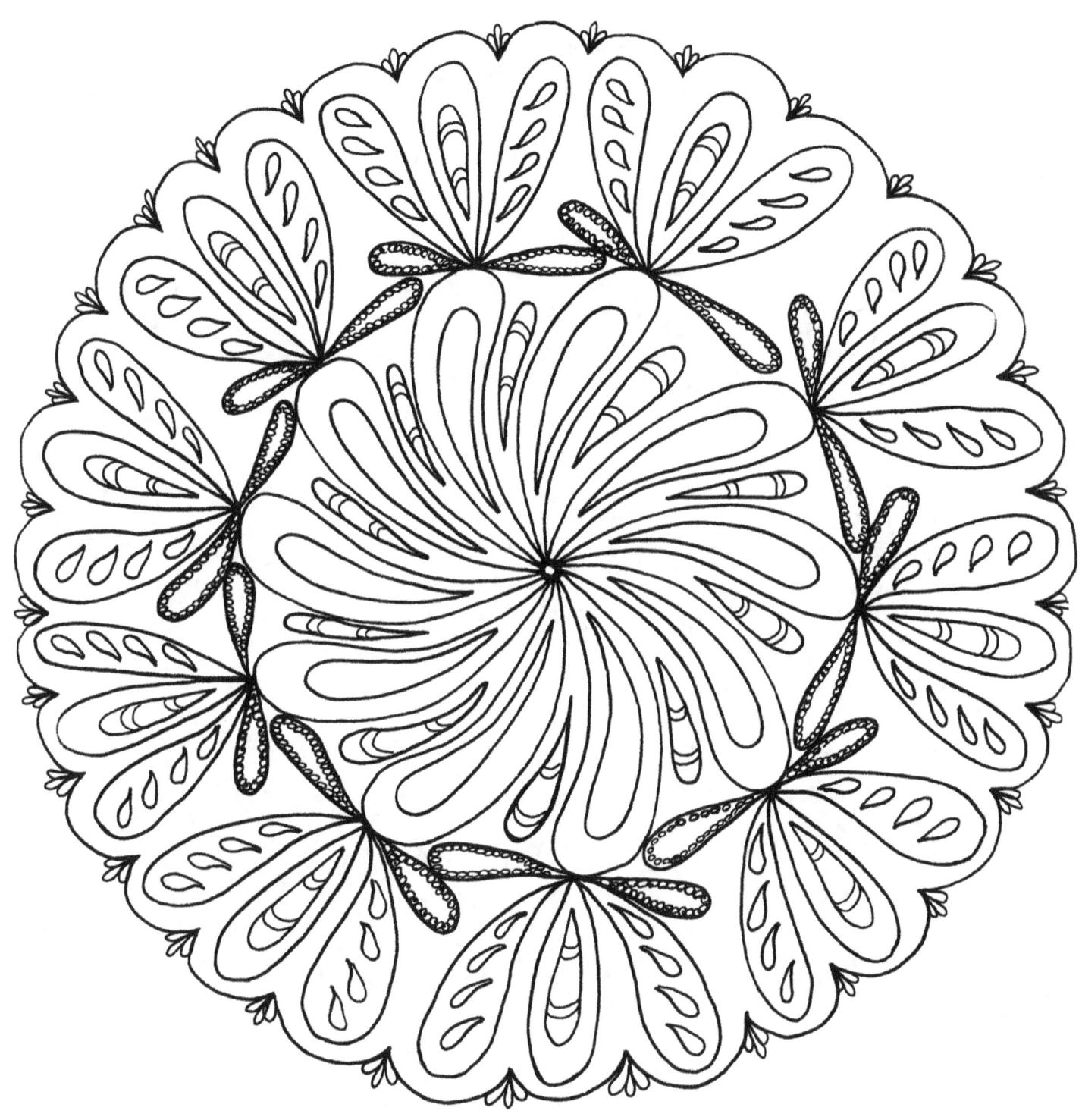

Contributing Artist
Nicole Whelan (Willow Hill Art)
WI, USA

Facebook : WillowHillArt
Etsy shop : WillowHillArt

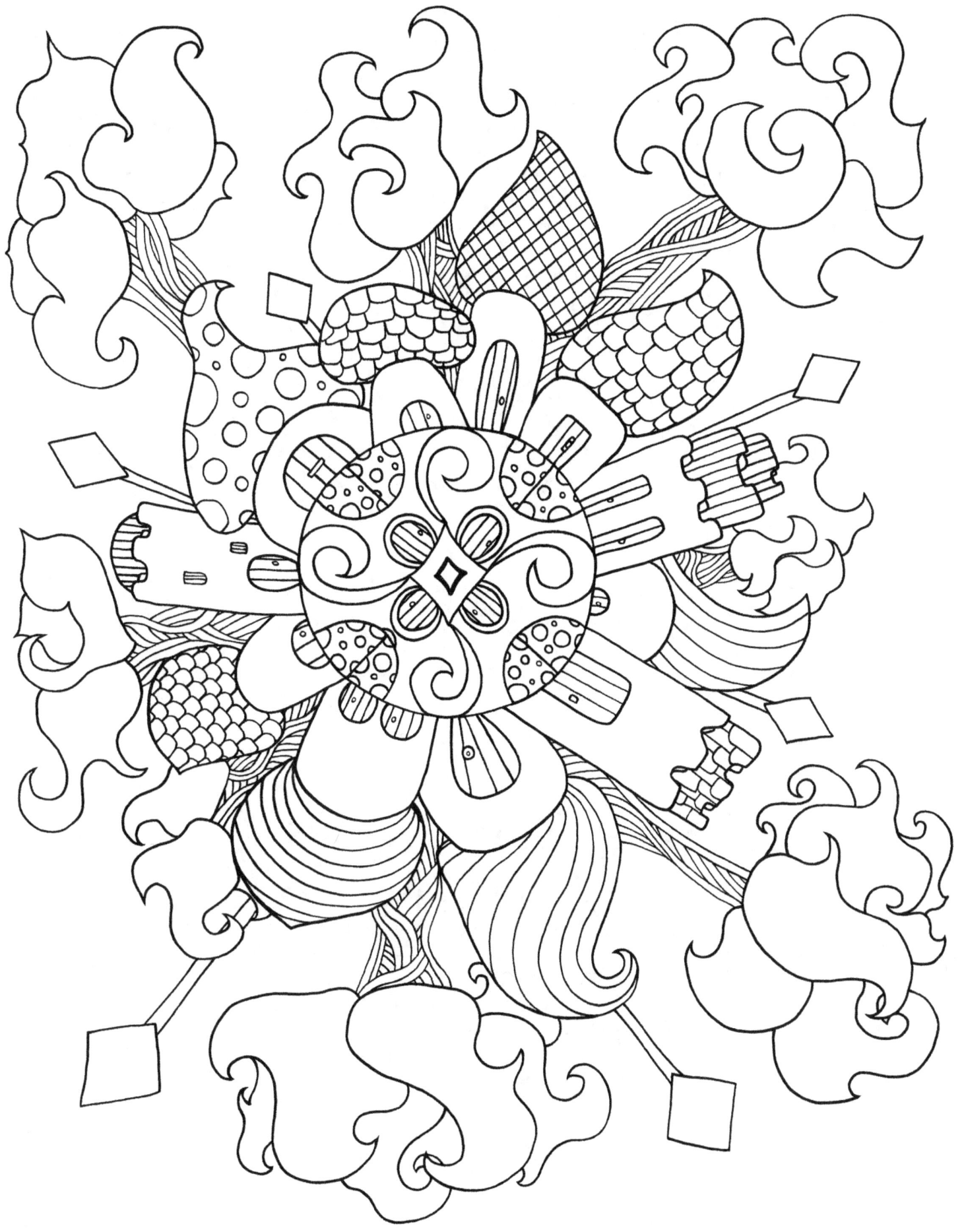

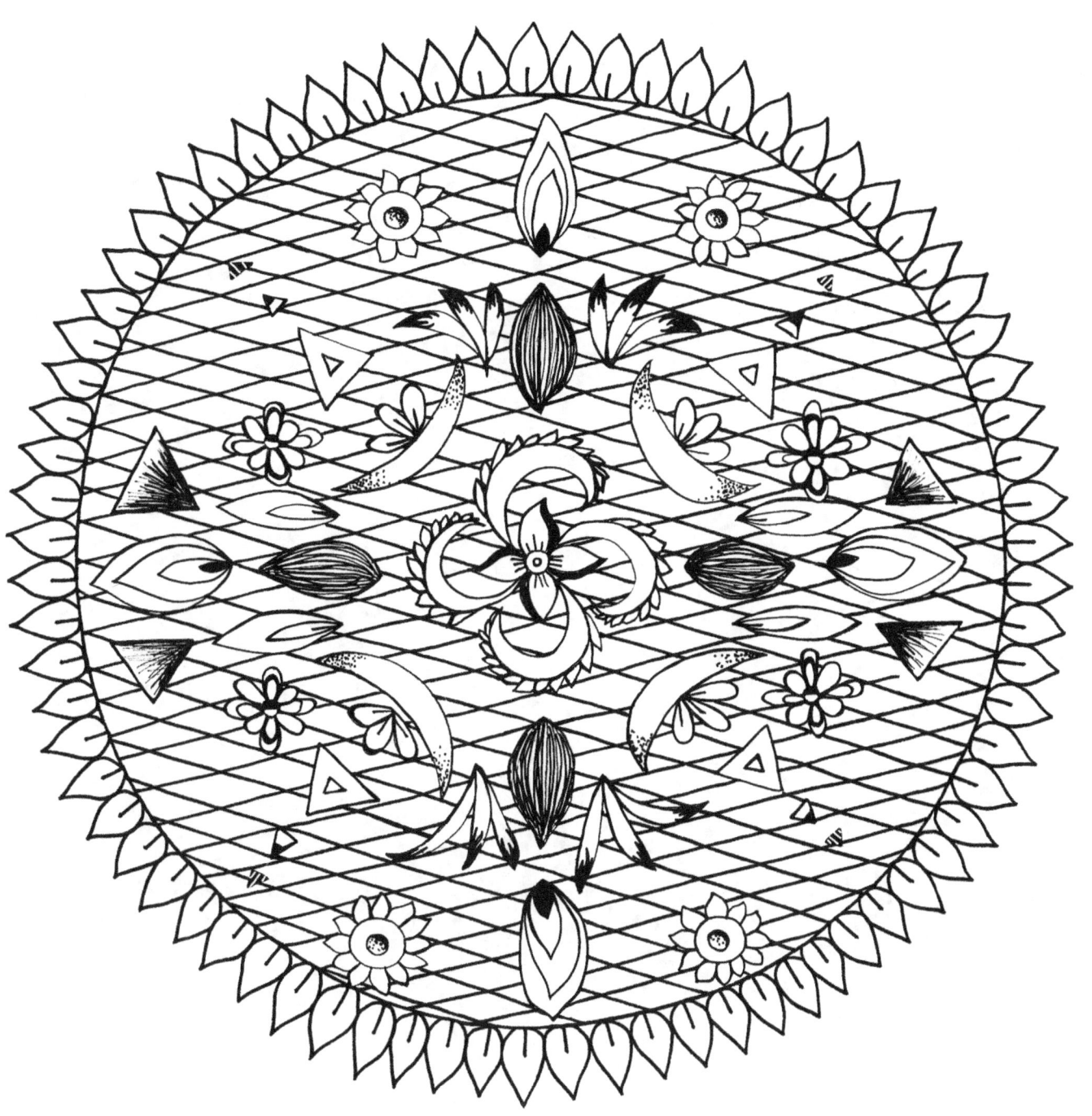

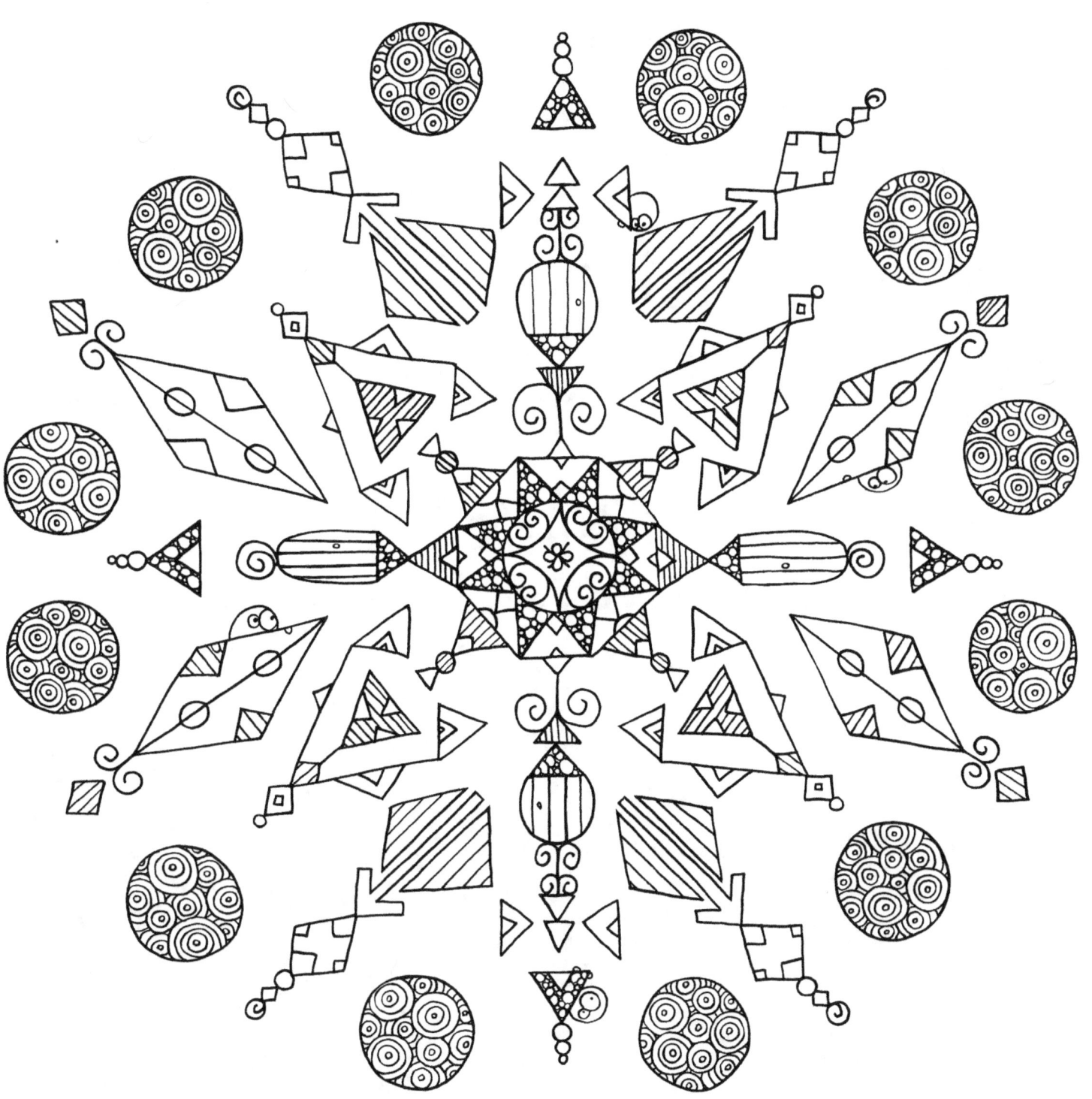

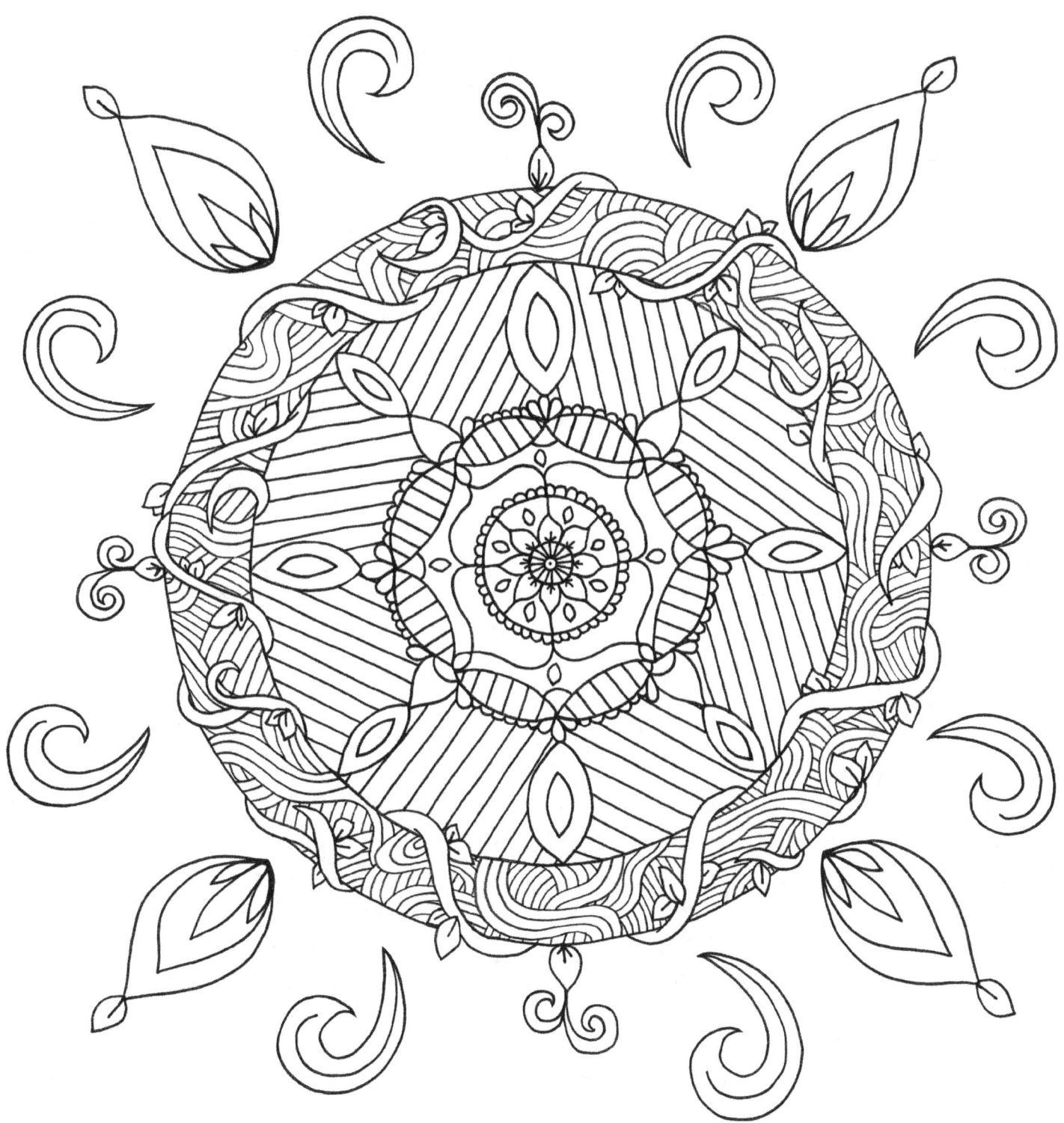

Contributing Artist
Mireille Westerduin, Colour by Mi
The Netherlands

Facebook : Colour-by-Mi-Kleurplaten-Illustraties

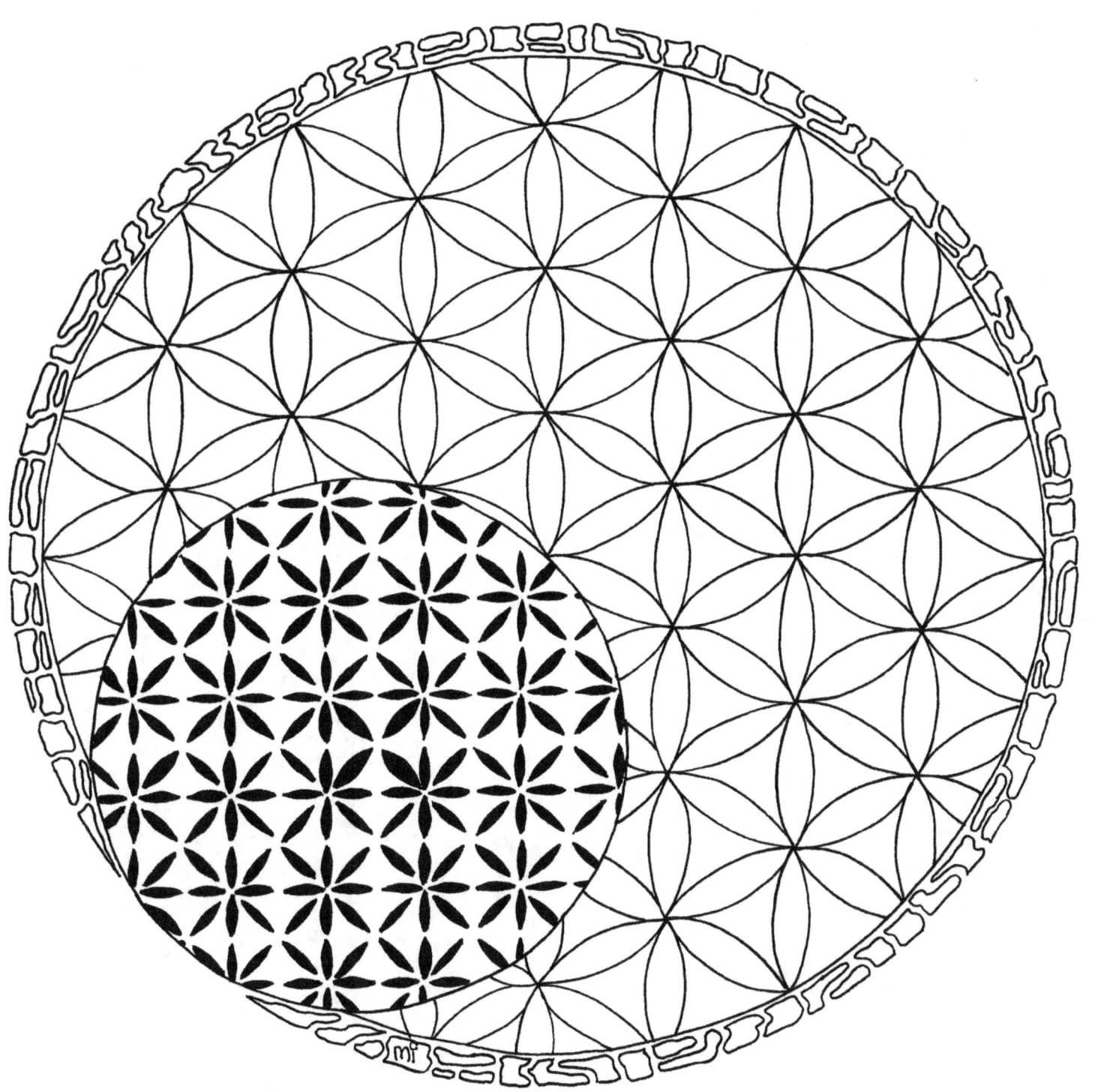

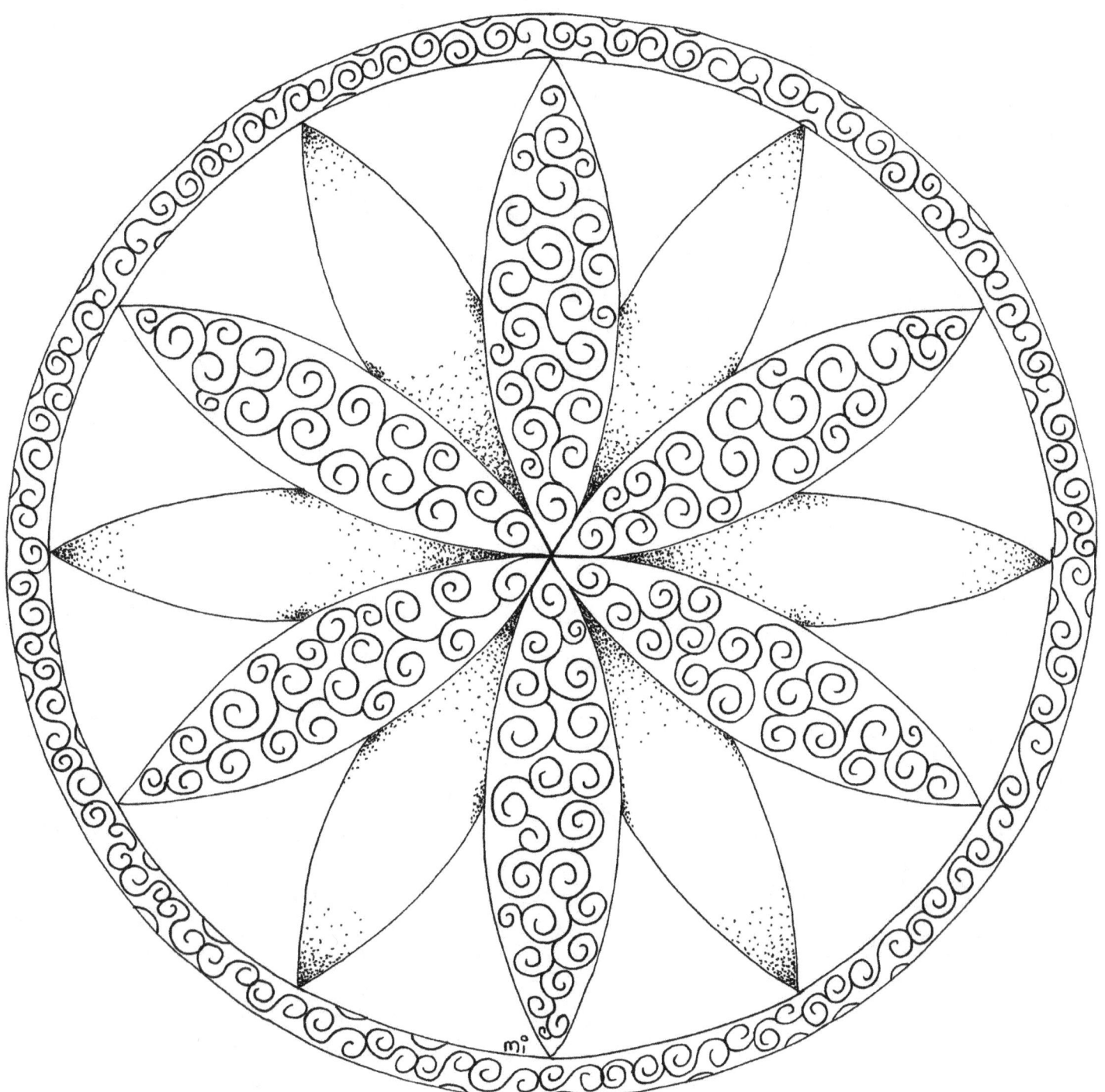

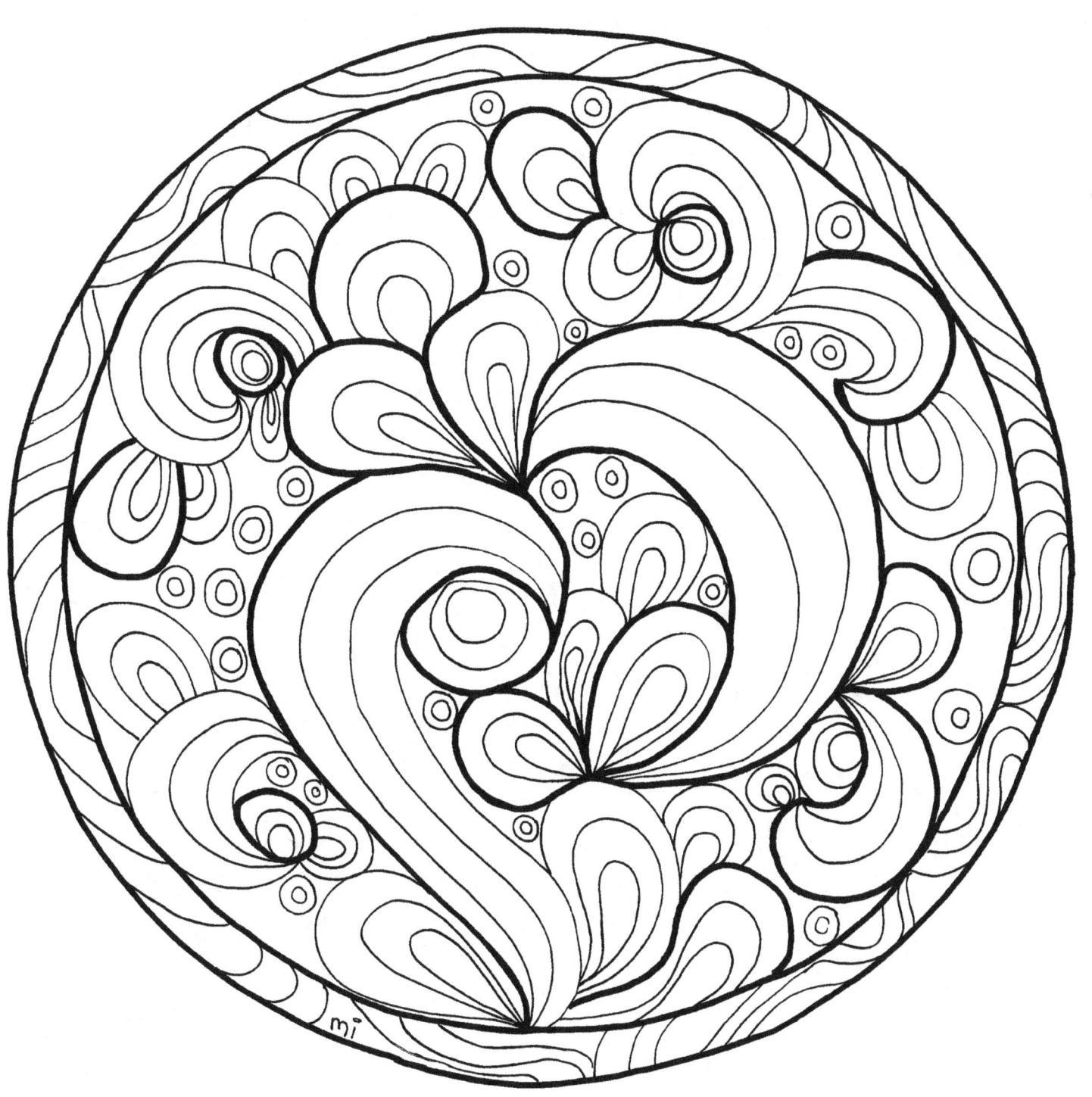

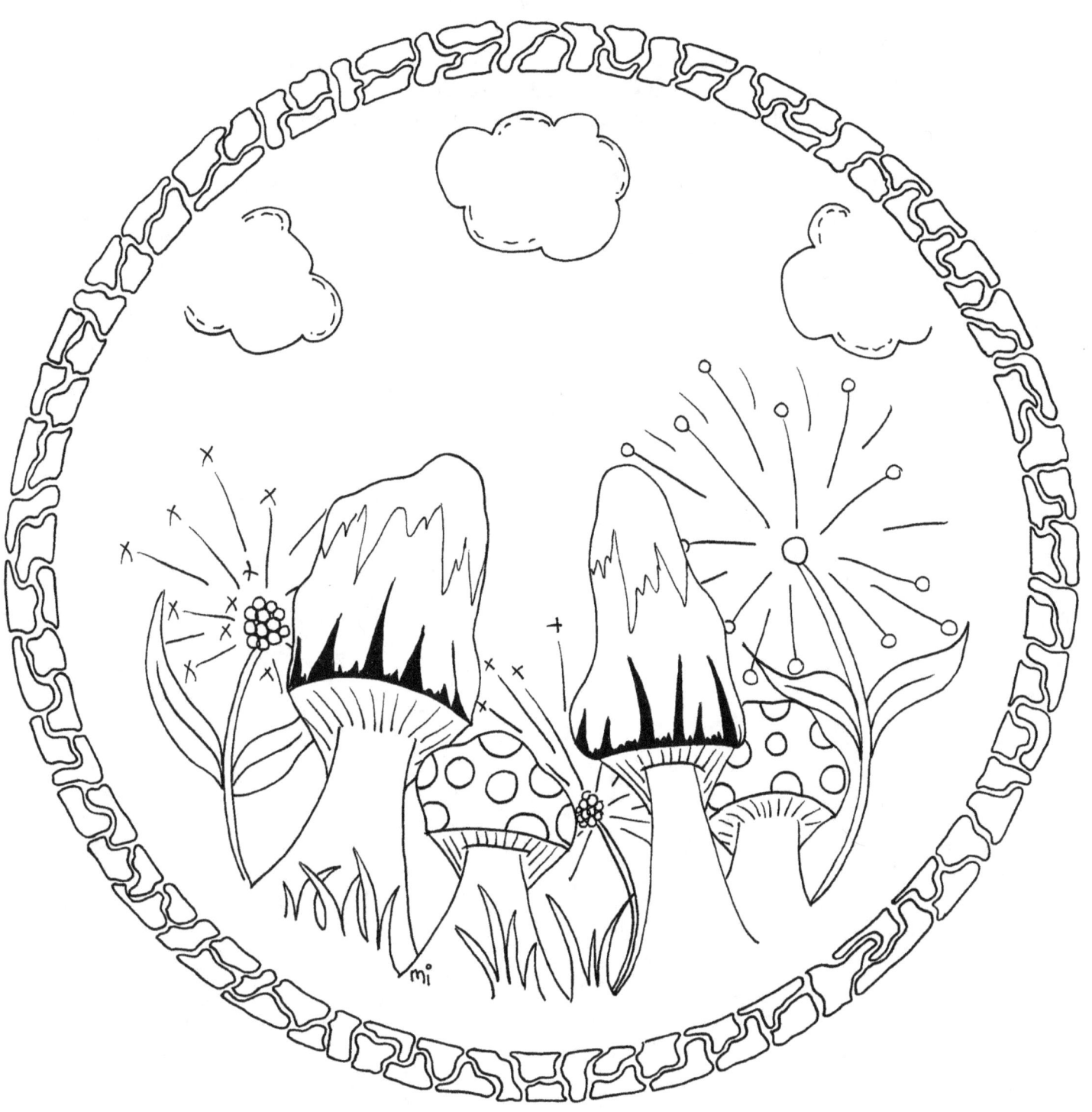

Contributing Artist
Ellen Wolters
The Netherlands

http://www.tekenpraktijkdeinnerlijkewereld.blogspot.nl/
http://ellenstraties.blogspot.nl/
https://www.youtube.com/user/DIWEllenWolters

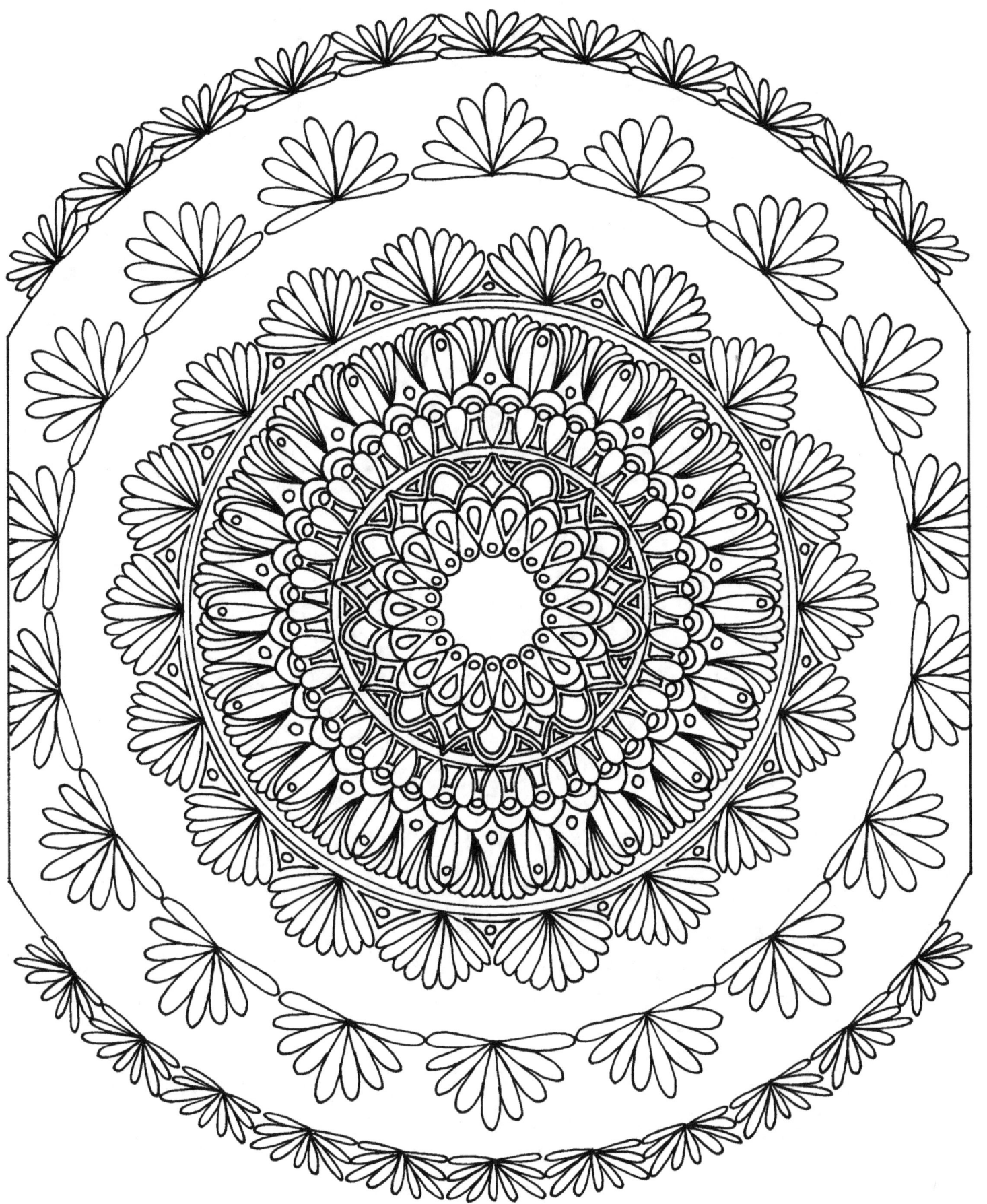

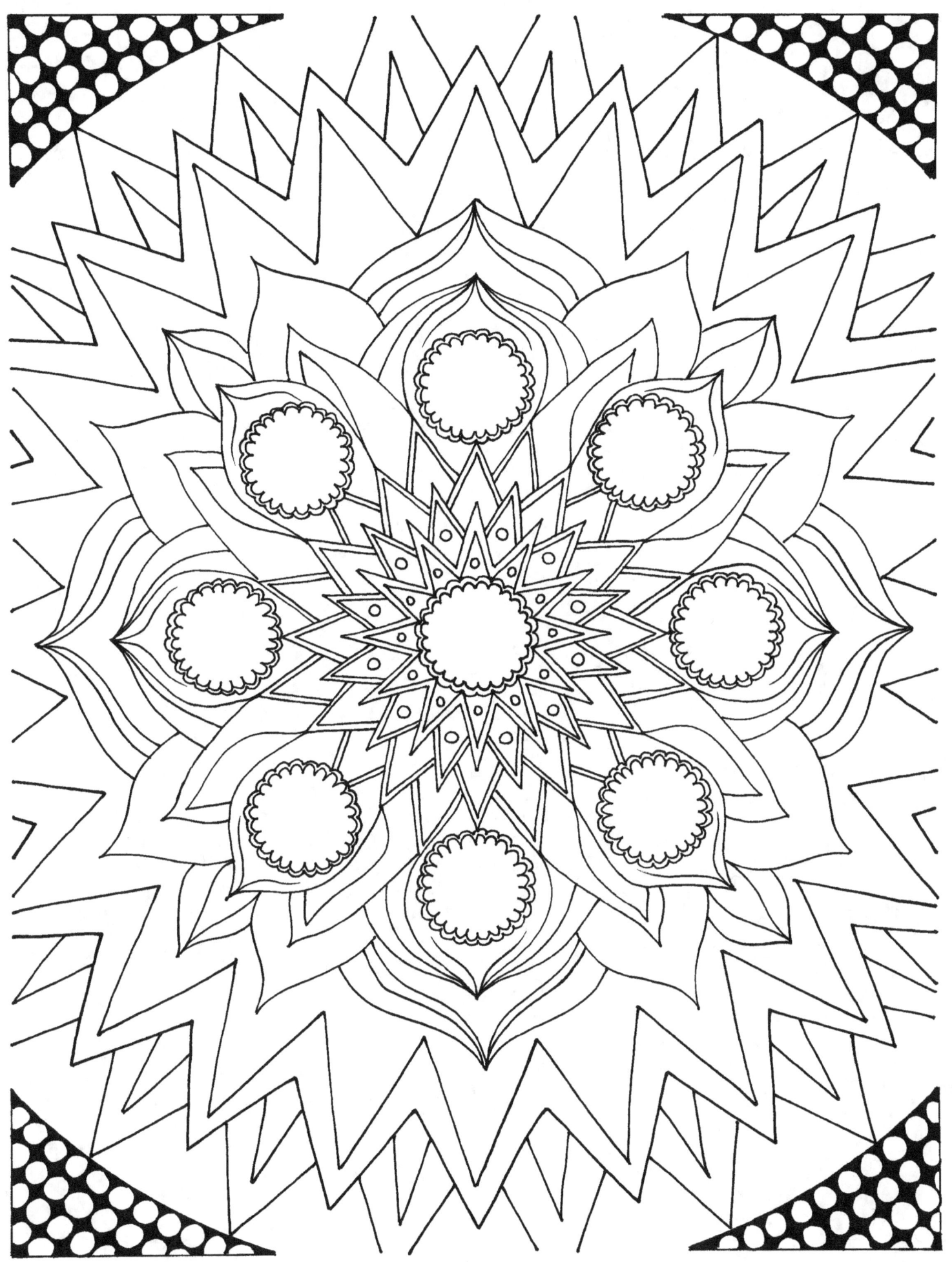

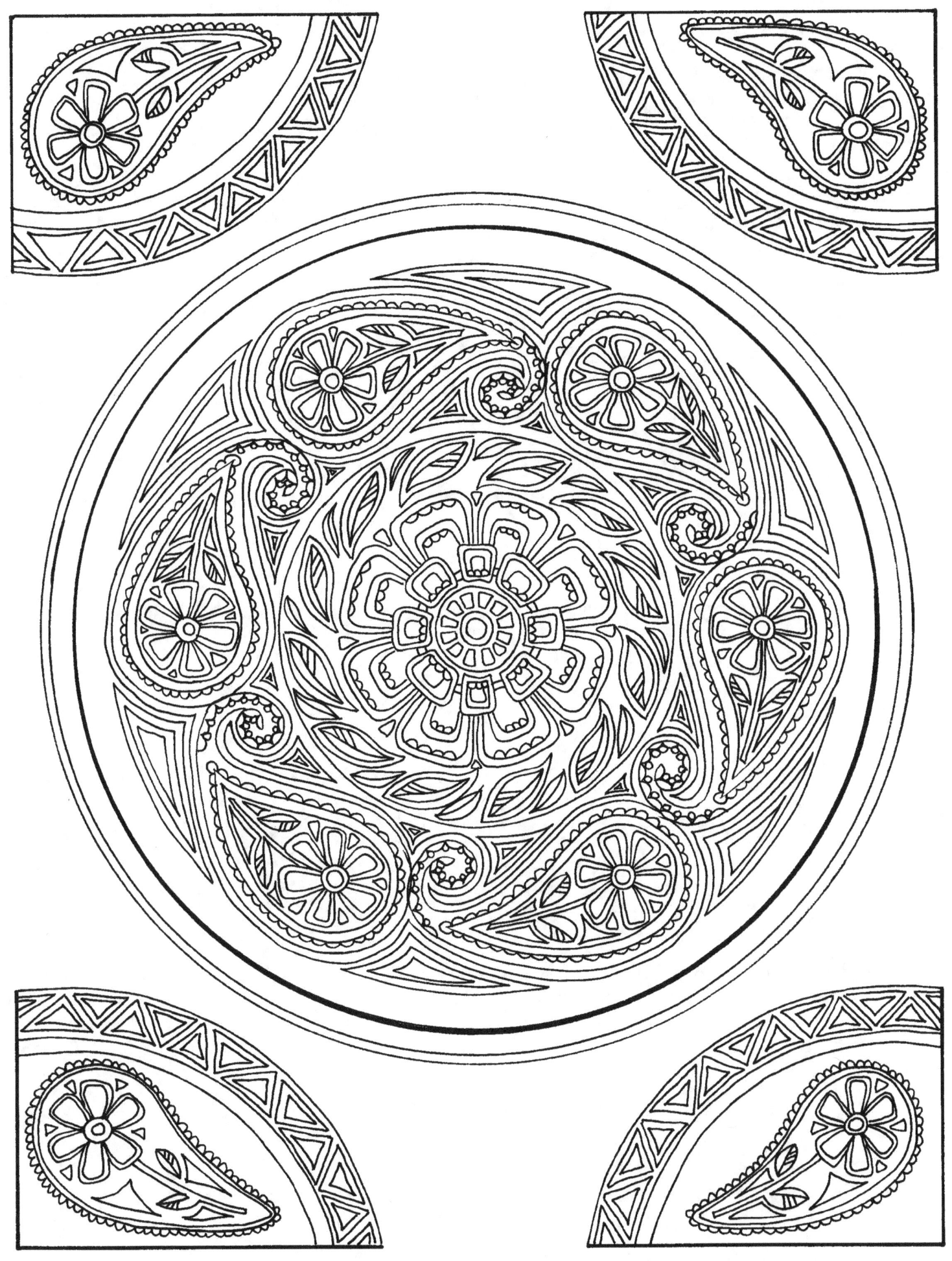

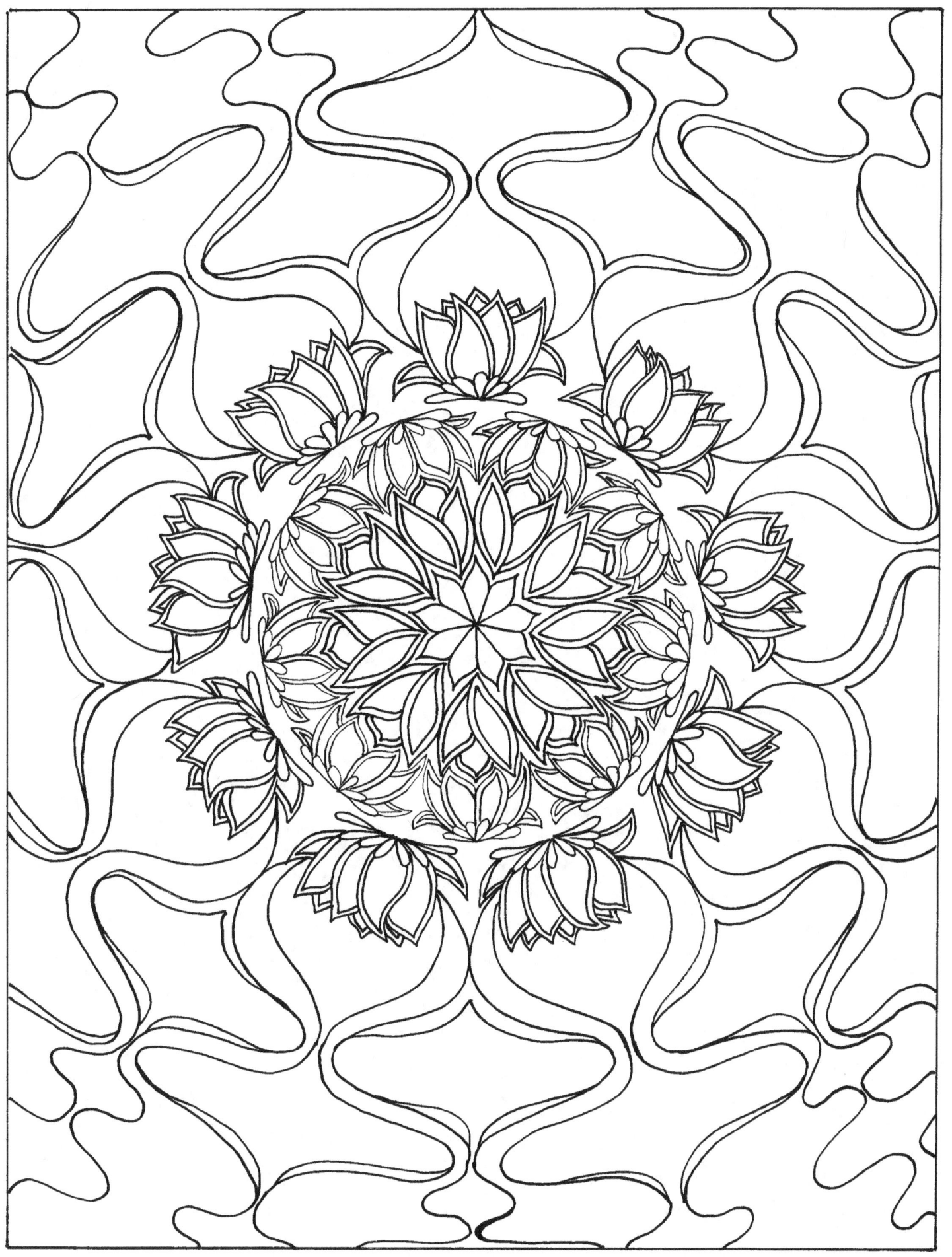

Drawn & colored by Gemeta Ling	Drawn & colored by DomDomx	Drawn & colored by Johanna Ans
Drawn & colored by Lynne McGee	Drawn & colored by TJ	Drawn & colored by Pica Wu
Drawn by Ahmed Fouad & colored by Ellen Wolters	Drawn & colored by Rover	Drawn by Yaya & colored by Martine Marguerat
Drawn & colored by Marieke Raterman-Bos	Drawn & colored by Dawn Miller	Drawn & colored by Audrey Sagh
Drawn & colored by Nicole Whelan	Drawn & colored by Mireille Westerduin, Colour by Mi	Drawn & colored by Ellen Wolters

www.ingramcontent.com/pod-product-compliance
Lightning Source LLC
Chambersburg PA
CBHW082208220526
45470CB00010B/3090